CORONATION
EVEREST

CORONATION
EVEREST

Jan Morris

BURFORD BOOKS

Printed in the United States of America.

10 9 8 7 6 5 4 3 2 1

Library of Congress Cataloging-in-Publication Data
Morris, James, 1926–
    Coronation Everest / by James Morris.
        p.   cm.
    Originally published: London : Faber & Faber, 1958.
    ISBN 1-58080-047-5
    1. Mount Everest Expedition (1953).   2. Reporters and reporting.
3. Hillary, Edmund, Sir.   4. Mountaineers—New Zealand—
Biography.   5. Times (London, England).   I. Title.
GV199.44.E85   M66   2000
796.52'2'092—dc21
    [B]   99-059691

Contents

Introduction
to the 2000 Edition

THIS LITTLE BOOK is a work of historical romanticism. It recalls the almost simultaneous occurrence of two events—a young queen's Coronation and the first ascent of a mountain—which profoundly stirred the world nearly fifty years ago. The queen was Elizabeth II of England. The mountain was Mount Everest, the highest of them all, climbed at last by a British expedition after decades of failed attempts.

It is hard to imagine now the almost mystical delight with which the coincidence of the two happenings was greeted in Britain itself. Emerging at last from the austerity which had plagued them since the Second World War, but at the same time facing the loss of their great Empire and the inevitable decline of their power in the world, the British people had half-convinced themselves that the accession of the young queen was a token of a fresh start—a new Elizabethan age, as the newspapers liked to call it. Coronation Day, June 2, 1953, was to be a day of symbolic hope and rejoicing, in which all the British patriotic loyalties would find a supreme moment of expression: and marvel of marvels, on that very day there arrived the news from distant places—from the frontiers of the old Empire, in fact—that a British team of mountaineers, led by a British soldier, Colonel John Hunt, had reached the supreme remaining earthly objective of exploration and adventure, the top of the world.

Things were different then. On the one hand space travel was yet to come, and the ascent of Mount Everest, since climbed by hundreds of people of all nationalities, was enough to thrill everyone. On the other hand the British monarchy was at an apex of its popularity. The moment aroused a whole orchestra of rich emotions among the British—pride, patriotism, nostalgia for the lost past of war and derring-do, hope for a rejuvenated future, satisfaction that Everest, essentially a British sphere of influence (as the old imperialists would have said), had been first climbed, as it should be, by the British. People of a certain age remember vividly to this day the moment when, as they waited on a drizzly June morning for the Coronation procession to pass by in London, they heard the magical news that the summit of the world was, so to speak, theirs. They cheered and sang as the news spread around the waiting crowds, and went on to ring the world.

Very improbably, for I am a lifelong republican, I was the newspaper correspondent who arranged this happy conjunction, and *Coronation Everest* explains how it happened. The book, which I wrote in the 1950s, needs to be read with a strong dose of historical sympathy, for everything has changed since then. I have changed myself—I was living and working as James Morris in those days—but Britain and the world have changed hardly less. Few such moments now could be accepted around the globe with such generous and uncomplicated pleasure. It was as though the celebrations of a family were infectious, and were shared by other peoples everywhere. Nearly half a century later, wherever I go someone is sure to raise the subject of my association with Everest and the Coronation, and they nearly always speak of it in a tone of wistful affection, as a memory from simpler times.

So please treat *Coronation Everest* with indulgence. Its excitements are those of long ago, and so are many of its attitudes.

—JAN MORRIS
Trefan Morys, Wales, 1999

For
HENRY MORRIS
born on page 107
and for the ones
who have climbed on

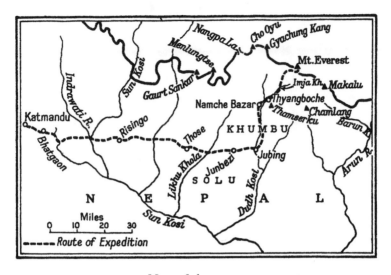

Map of the route

The environs of Everest

The News Reaches London

ON THE EVE of Queen Elizabeth's Coronation, June 1, 1953, there arrived in London the news that Mount Everest, the supreme mountain, had been climbed for the first time, and by a British expedition. The last of the great terrestrial objectives was reached; the way was clear for the earth satellites and the moon rockets. Of all the marvellous Coronation gifts, this was the most glittering. The huge crowds, waiting all night in the drizzly streets to see the queen pass by, cheered and sang when they heard the news, and the newspaper editors hurriedly remade their editions. In Buckingham Palace the queen's private secretary, Sir Alan Lascelles, heard by telephone from *The Times* of London, and the queen herself learnt of the triumph through the medium of one of the dignified red dispatch boxes by which affairs of state are communicated to Her Majesty. 'It helped us to sleep that night,' remarked the Duke of Edinburgh, 'what little sleep we got!'

Within minutes the news was around the world, and an extraordinary wave of delight and excitement ran across the continents. 'A thumping victory over the King of Adventure!' proclaimed an Indian official in Nepal. 'The unconquerable has been conquered,' said the *New York Times*. In the annexe of Westminster Abbey, as the begowned and ruffled dignitaries prepared themselves for the Coronation service, Field-Marshal Lord Montgomery of Alamein was seen to be reading about Everest in a newspaper; and in a million humbler hearts, everywhere, the announcement of the great ascent struck a spark of especial pride that Coronation morning.

This small book is the story of the news from Everest, and how it travelled from the summit of the mountain to England in time to coincide so miraculously with the day of celebration. There have perhaps been greater adventures than Everest (and there are certainly greater to come); but none have culminated so romantically—the two small figures on the summit linked by such devious means with the trumpets, the golden coaches, the splendid gowns, the heralds, and all the feudal pomp and ceremony of Coronation London. Drake himself could not have timed his gallantries more grandly; and history will perhaps always associate Coronation Day—June 2, 1953—with both great mountains and magnificent monarchies.

1

Theory

POOR EVEREST was not always 'news'. In the old days an assault on the highest of peaks was an adventure for gentlemen, tarnished by no cheap nationalist ambition, unspoilt by the stridencies of publicity. An Everest expedition was a group of English sportsmen, attended by their native servants, trying to climb an impossibly difficult hill in a ludicrously distant place, and quietly risking their lives in doing so. The world did not watch their efforts with any feverish interest. No global factions arose in support of this or that climber, to denigrate the European or elevate the Asiatic, to seize upon chance remarks or passing squabbles as material for scandal. Ten British expeditions went to Everest before the Second World War, and except for a sad romantic aura that surrounded the disappearance of Irvine and Mallory, no element of passion pursued their attempts. The great public was, by the frenetic standards of today, not much interested.

There was, however, an audience of mountaineers, adventurers, and sympathizers who looked on with technical or scholarly concern and who contributed (often with a sudden and eccentric gusto) to such controversies as that arising from the use of artificial aids to climbing. A fragrance of English oddness is left to us from those early expeditions. The Abominable Snowman first made his appearance not as a figure of vulgar fun, or material for scientists, but rather as a strange squire of the snows, moving sedately if a little lumpishly through his remote estate. Many of the climbers were notable for pungency of wit, splendid independence, or colourful bigness. Everest had not been cheapened or distorted, and those who climbed upon it formed an exclusive society of adventurers.

One London newspaper, *The Times,* was particularly concerned with the venture from the beginning. In return for financial backing, it secured the copyright of dispatches from almost all the pre-war expeditions, and became the accepted channel of information from the mountain at a time when most other papers took little serious notice. The leader of each expedition undertook, as part of his duties, to 'write the dispatches for *The Times*'. There was no hectic newsroom flavour to this kind of journalism. From time to time the mountaineer would collect his writing materials about him, closing the flap of his tent to keep out the wind, and settle down to describe the progress of the attempt, much as he might write to complain about the pollution of a trout stream, or invite contributions to some charitable fund. Graceful and entertaining was the writing of most of these climbers, marred by no Fleet Street clichés, with no axes to grind and only the gentlest of trumpets to blow.

Alas, by 1953, when Sir John Hunt's triumphant expedition was completing its preparations in England, all had changed. The powers of Europe had been humbled by war, and in their silly efforts to prove themselves still important had revived the concept of sport as a medium of nationalist fervour. People no longer went to the Himalaya only for the fun of it. The French had climbed Annapurna with a flourish of national pride. The Swiss, more jingoistic than one would suppose from their circumstances, made two brave attempts on Everest, and nearly climbed it. In a first slight whiff of publicity people were beginning to call Everest 'the British mountain', just as they called Nanga Parbat 'the German mountains'. Moreover, Hunt was going to Everest in Coronation Year—a year fondly hailed by the press, on the flimsiest of evidence, as the beginning of a new Elizabethan era—and it was difficult for an Englishman, however enlightened, to stifle the thought that a British success on the mountain would be a most suitable Coronation offering. Long before the expedition set out there was therefore a rumble of interest and expectation.

The Times, on whose editorial staff I then proudly worked, again had the copyright to dispatches from the expedition; but it could clearly no longer afford to rely upon climbers' journalism, produced when opportunity offered in the knowledge that only one newspaper was really concerned. This time there would be strong competition for the story, fanned by nationalist sentiment and honest patriotic pride, even fostered by the two current cold wars—between Capitalism and Communism, between East and West. It became obvious to everyone that this time the Everest party must (swallowing its natural revulsion) include in its number a professional journalist, concerned only with the problems of getting the news home to England. Nobody much liked the idea, if only because the expedition was big enough already; but Hunt, kindliest of commanders, digested the fact that I had never set foot on a mountain before and even summoned up a wan smile as, over lunch one day at the Garrick Club, he invited me to join his team as special correspondent of *The Times.*

The chief problem was not how to secure the news, but how to relay it back to London. Everest was one of the less accessible of the great mountains, partly because fairly harsh physical barriers blocked most routes to it, chiefly because of the political peculiarities of its situation. It lay exactly on the frontier between two countries of secretive tradition. To the north was Tibet, shrouded alike in Buddhist mysticism and Communist suspicion, and in 1953 more firmly closed to Westerners than ever; to the south Nepal, a medieval kingdom, slowly opening like a warmed bud to permit the entrance of foreign ideas and values. Bang on the line that divided these two theatrical states lay Everest, and the frontier (according to the map) crossed its very summit, more than 29,000 feet above the sea.

Since the war the way to Everest had necessarily lain through Nepal, whose rulers were generally obliging and whose myriads of poor labourers welcomed the work of porterage. You could conveniently fly into Katmandu from India (any good Piccadilly travel agent would book you a ticket there) and in that strange city you could engage your porters and buy many of the smaller necessities of mountain life. There was a British Embassy, and an Indian Embassy, and some Americans, and a cable office which sent its messages to India by radio for onward transmission to Europe. Once you left Katmandu, though, the temptations of civilization were nearly all behind you. No road led to Everest. Outside the valley of Katmandu there were no wheeled vehicles in Nepal, and only a meagre series of rough tracks crossed the hilly hinterland, connecting the golden capital with Tibet, Sikkim, and the north. To get anywhere inside Nepal you must walk, for even ponies were scarce, and many of the tracks were too narrow, precipitous, and forbidding for easy horsemanship. Patient porters carried your bags for you, and clasping your pins to your bosom you must trudge your way through the hills, dazzled by the alpine flowers, inspired by the distant white snow peaks, slightly befuddled by the local liquor, feeling like some antique Mandarin, excessively influential, journeying through the Chinese uplands for a parley with Marco Polo.

By these stately means it took ten days or more to travel from Katmandu to Everest. The track crossed the grain of the country, as the geographers say, as if it had deliberately chosen to intersect contours rather than follow them. Sometimes it descended into impenetrable gorges; sometimes it crossed high mountain ranges; and although it was a pleasant journey, enlivened by all kinds of unusual interests, it was not the kind of route you would wish to follow too often in a hurry.

This was to be the supply route of the expedition, and the way its members marched to the mountain. More to my point, all this rugged, primitive country, hard and wheel-less, lay between the mountain and the nearest cable office. The foreign correspondent is never happy if he is far from a telephone or a cable-head, and it was daunting to envisage this 200 miles of intervening country without the saving grace of a single post office.

How the gap could be bridged was therefore my first preoccupation, for the news had to travel not only safely, but swiftly too. Radio was the obvious answer, but though the Nepalese authorities were both helpful and sympathetic, they were understandably chary of allowing powerful radio transmitters to be operated so near their northern frontiers. All kinds of other methods were proposed. Some people suggested carrier pigeons, others beacon fires. Some said that since the Buddhist priests of the Everest region had remarkable telepathic powers, they might be willing simply to think the news away. There was a scheme to float news dispatches in cellophane containers down a river that happens to flow from the Everest area into India; where some unfortunate helper, it was proposed, would stand poised upon the bank, like a destitute angler, waiting for a package to appear.

None of these proposals seemed altogether satisfactory, though the beacon fires certainly had a genuine Elizabethan allure; and in the end it seemed that despite all the miracles of modern science, my dispatches would have to be sent back to Katmandu by runner. This at least was a well-tried method. Earlier Everest expeditions had always employed such men, and Hunt would have a number of them to take his own messages and convey the mail. I would probably need to recruit another small corps of my own. If the runners were well paid and kindly treated, they would probably see to it (I thought) that dispatches were in the cable office on the tenth or eleventh day after leaving the mountain.

So the plan was arranged. I was to go to Everest with a rearguard party, led by Major J. O. M. Roberts, which would follow the expedition proper with supplies of oxygen. Another correspondent of *The Times*, Arthur Hutchinson, would be stationed in Katmandu to receive messages, interpret and supplement them where necessary, and shepherd them through the cablehead. There was, however, always the possibility that other newspapers would send men out to Nepal too, to intercept or steal our messages and grasp what news they could. Just how ruthless they would be, nobody knew. Would they lurk behind boulders with clubs, waiting to pounce upon our runners? Or would they merely bribe the cable office to divulge or delay our messages?

It seemed foolish to take risks. It was not so much that other papers should not have the news as well as *The Times;* more serious was the possibility that they would succeed in publishing it *before The Times* (and the many foreign newspapers associated with it)—that we would be scooped on our own story. So some alternative routes were arranged. From Everest another rough track ran to the south across the Indian frontier, through the appalling jungle country of the Terai, to a small town called

Jogbani, where there was a cable office. There an agent would be stationed, so that if the Katmandu route seemed insecure, runners could go southwards instead. There was even a third alternative. When the Swiss were on Everest in the preceding year, they sent their messages to Europe through the medium of a Jesuit priest living at Patna, a large Indian city in the province of Bihar, which runners could reach by taking a narrow-gauge railway from the frontier. We would again try to enlist the help, we decided, of this adaptable priest.

But supposing the runners were actually intercepted en route, or the cable office at Katmandu proved easily bribable? It would obviously be impracticable to encode the whole of long descriptive messages from the mountain, even if they recorded some particular stage in the course of the attempt. But there was no reason why we should not devise code words to disguise personal names, certain key events, places on the mountainside, and altitudes. So a code card was produced, printed on waterproofed cardboard in the touching faith that we would be constantly pulling it from the pockets of our windproofs in the teeth of monstrous gales and stinging blizzards. I am no cipherer, and I was chiefly concerned, in evolving this simple system, in giving a deadpan or enigmatic air to things; and indeed it is marvellous how poker-faced the language can be if you give thought to it. The alternative code words for John Hunt, for example, were 'Kettle' and 'Stringbag'. Wilfrid Noyce, another climber, was 'Radiator' or 'Windowsill'. Three thousand feet came out as 'Waistcoat Crossword Amsterdam', and the mountain's sublime summit, home of myths and deities, was christened 'Golliwog'. There were snags to such a code. Once enciphered, a message was nonsense, thus making it apparent that something significant was being concealed; and it might be necessary to be especially nice to the cable authorities to induce them to transmit such a stream of gibberish.

I would send these messages back to Katmandu in pad-locked canvas bags, or perhaps in the stitched fabric envelopes provided to contain the expedition's exposed films. Once there, Hutchinson would see that the news was sent on expeditely to London. It all sounded splendid old-fashioned journalism, in the true cleft-stick tradition; and packing a new ribbon for my typewriter, and collecting my corduroy trousers from the cleaners, I flew gaily off one morning to India.

2

Preparation

A NARROW GORGE in the mountains was the gate to Katmandu, and through this forbidding portal the airplane from India must pass. Eddies and swirls of air bumped the machine about, and on either side the high mountain crags rose high above us. This was a true frontier. Behind lay India, a familiar and friendly place, where you could buy the *Illustrated London News;* in front was Nepal, until a few years before one of the least known of all the countries of the earth, and in 1953 still haunted by lingering wraiths of mystery. I had done my necessary business in India—collected a tent in Delhi, called on our Jesuit priest at Patna, bought some pots and pans and carbon paper. In Katmandu my adventure would begin.

There is always something fascinating about a great city secluded among mountains, and Katmandu, seen from the air for the first time, glittering in the hard sunshine, with the glorious peaks of the high Himalaya standing behind it, was a splendid and genuinely exotic sight. The wide valley that surrounded it was dazzlingly green, with vivid patches of yellow and red marking the cultivation of some especially improbable vegetable. Wooded foothills ran towards the capital from the high mountains, and a river of crystal blue wandered through the flat country and bisected the city. Against this heavenly background stood Katmandu, a complex of temples and towers and palaces, with a distinct sense of lunacy about it.

In 1953 there was no road into Katmandu, and all the precarious motor vehicles tottering through its streets had been manhandled there on the backs of innumerable coolies; on the track that crossed the mountains from India it was never surprising to encounter a company of a hundred raggedy porters carrying a monumental Rolls-Royce without any wheels. There was no railway line, either, the only method of ground communication being a rope railway which constantly heaved tinned food and spare carburettors over the hills from Bihar. The airplane came in once or twice a week, keeping its fingers crossed (for it is a difficult flight), and many visitors plodded over the pass from India on ponies. In general, though, despite the rapid unfolding of Nepalese policy, Katmandu still felt isolated, introspective, and auspicious.

Nepal was in a condition of gradual revolution. The great families which used to control the hereditary prime ministership (and thereby, as may be imagined, a fair number of other jobs too) had been humbled, and a sort of democratic society functioned intermittently, with many a splutter and spurt. There were political parties and newspapers and a lively radio station, and the British reading room was allowed to display even the most scurrilous of the Sunday theatre criticisms. Strange indeed were the people who moved through the dusty streets of Katmandu. Sometimes a prime minister rushed along in his big limousine, with his fierce attendant policemen; sometimes a gaunt holy man stalked through the crowd ominously.

Tibetans in their queer clothes and long black hair squatted beside the road chatting; beggars intoned their stylized whimpering appeals; the occasional European climber bought his last requirements in the open-fronted (but scarcely open-hearted) shops of the big bazaar. It was at once colourful and squalid. Some of the people were handsome and well dressed, but most of them lived in unutterable poverty; and the whole strange medley was infused with an unhealthy sense of distrust.

I felt the impact of this trait very soon during my short stay in Katmandu. I had taken my bags from the airport to the Nepal Hotel, a defunct palace of incomparable discomfort then used as a rest-house for visitors. It was a huge structure, formerly the home of some grandee of consequence, and filled to overflowing with bric-a-brac—stuffed tigers locked in eternal combat, pictures of Nepalese noblemen in dramatic uniforms, mats bearing the emblazoned slogan 'Welcome!', embroidered mottoes such as 'Bless This House' or 'East West, Home's Best', fading photographs of elephant hunts, banquets, obscure state occasions, and kings. In the great courtyard strutted the chickens which later appeared in heart-rending regularity upon the dinner table. In the bar a jazz band played a confusing mixture of Nepalese and American music, the double-bass player being an elegant Nepalese lady in horn-rimmed spectacles; sometimes in the early morning the pianist, who used to play in ship's orchestras on the run between England and India, would sneak into the room to practice his Chopin.

Often one could hear through one's bedroom window the cries of wild animals: an apologetic lion's roar, the cluckings of hidden birds. These noises came from a zoo in a charming but derelict garden directly opposite the hotel. I once visited this menagerie, and found it strangely fascinating. It had been the private property of a nobleman driven from the country by the onslaught of democracy, and it was maintained in a state of semi-coma by the city of Katmandu. Everything was a little overgrown and weedy. The lions were heavy with boredom. The tigers were moulting. The biggest python, tired of it all, had escaped. The pelican flapped grotesquely up and down the lawns with a half-hearted beating of his clipped wings. On one cage I saw a notice saying 'Gibbon'; but inside there was only a solitary parrot, and as I approached I heard a furtive scurrying and sliding, and there vanished into the recesses of the cage a score of small brown rats, which had been clinging to the mesh-work examining that unhappy bird. This melancholy place exactly fitted the temperament of the Nepal Hotel, which was, all in all, an unusual hostelry.

Soon after my arrival, without unpacking my bags, I set off down the road to see the town. It was a long walk down a narrow street, between the high uncompromising walls of palaces (now and again, through wrought iron gates, you could glimpse the ornate facade of a pink chateau, transplanted in essence from the banks of the Loire but subjected in the process to some ghastly spiritual metamorphosis). It was hot and dusty, and the people I met on the street were mostly dirty and unsmiling. Presently I heard the roar of an engine behind me and a jeep pulled up in an insidious sort of way. It contained three important-looking gentlemen and a policeman.

'Good afternoon, Mr. Morris,' said one of them a little coldly. 'We have been looking after you since the hotel, it being our purpose to discover your whereabouts. This is His Highness the Maharajah of Rambledop' (or some such name) 'who is in Katmandu on a visit to one of his distinguished kinsmen. Have you by any chance seen the maharajah's suitcase—the brown one, with his princely crest on the lid?'

'I'm so sorry,' said I, 'but I really don't think I have.'

'Oh,' said the dignitary, and with a concerted bow in my direction, and an exchange of significant glances, the party drove off.

Such were the fascinations of Katmandu that I easily dismissed this little incident from my mind. Instead I wandered enthralled through the little back streets, filled with primitive perfumes, alive with a drifting crowd of diverse citizens. In the shops the merchants lay torpid on their blankets. Officials strode along in gorgeous uniforms, bright with medal ribbons, and Indian ladies rustled past in lovely saris. Sometimes a Nepalese soldier clattered down the pavement in ammunition boots. On the green grass of the central parade ground a group of aristocrats were exercising their stocky horses, riding with an unorthodox grace. A young man with an eye-glass was examining the workmanship of an horrific figure of the Hindu god Kala Bhaibar, which sprawled (all arms and eyes) beside the main square.

But from time to time, as I looked at these wonders, the jeep would draw up beside me disconcertingly.

'Our kindest apologies,' the spokesman would say, 'but we have once again been examining your whereabouts. His Highness the Maharajah of Rambledop graciously wonders if you have knowledge of the whereabouts of his brown leather suitcase, suitably emblazoned? No, sir? You have no knowledge, sir? Kindly accept my warm apologies.'

After a time, I confess, it began to tell on my nerves, particularly as Katmandu always had for me a slight sensation of creepiness. I visited the Buddhist shrine of Shambu-nath, shuddering as I passed through the settlement at its foot, for many of its inhabitants were albinos, looking at me eerily with pink eyes. At the top of the steep stairs of the shrine stood the tall *stupa*, surrounded by houses and monuments; scores of horrible hairy monkeys clambered over these structures and through the windows of the buildings; and the two large Oriental eyes which embellished the edifice seemed to stare at me with a decided air of accusation. *Had* I seen the maharajah's suitcase? Could I have made some terrible mistake?

I dismissed the idea, and set back along the road to the hotel; but in a moment or two the jeep was with me again.

'Our warmest apologies, but the maharajah graciously wonders if he might be permitted to inspect the baggage in your room, sir, with your warm permission?'

'Bother the beastly suitcase,' said I, or something of the sort. 'Yes, for goodness' sake come and see for yourself!' Chasing a respectable British subject around the back streets, I muttered as I climbed into the jeep, as if I haven't got enough to think about already, it's all this confounded nationalism, it just goes to show, etc. etc. etc.: until the key of my room was secured, there was a general catching of breaths and bracing of muscles, the door was flung theatrically open; and there in the middle of the floor stood a large brown suitcase, including in the convolutions of its monogram a number of crowns, sceptres, orbs, eagles, and other symbols of sovereignty.

'My goodness,' I said breathlessly, 'I *am* sorry!'

For a moment this characteristic episode seemed to threaten my entire Everest assignment. The maharajah opened his suitcase to show me, tucked away between a pair of pants and a toothpaste tube, a case of magnificent jewels which, he said convincingly, were most precious to him. It was obvious, he said, that the case had been in some way confused with my baggage at the airport; and since, as a marginal member of the Everest expedition, I had been immune to customs requirements, it had been hurried away into the city without examination. This seemed to me odd.

'Now I must insist,' said the maharajah, a steely note entering his voice, 'that you give me a signed explanation of the affair, kindly making it clear that you were (albeit unwillingly, my dear sir) responsible for bringing the case into the city.'

It all sounded rather fishy, but when I stood my ground and insisted, with a quivering forefinger, that he remove his possessions at once out of my room, it was gently suggested to me that the maharajah might well be in a position to prevent my going to the mountain. In a trice, I freely confess, I had written a brief but unliterary account of the episode and handed it to him with expressions of everlasting goodwill; but over the years I have often remembered the maharajah's jewels, and wondered at the strange way in which they passed through the customs.

A little nervous that something else of the sort might happen to me, I then set about completing my preparations for the march. Hutchinson was already in Katmandu, often secreted, during the hot hours of the day, in the innermost recesses of a blackened room, but already with a firm finger upon the pulse of the city. All our forebodings about the competition, he said, were coming true. Hunt and his climbers had left for Everest a week or so before, and were now half-way to the mountain; but they had been closely followed by an enterprising British correspondent, Ralph Izzard of the *Daily Mail*, who had boldly set off into the hills with a tattered tent and a scratch team of porters. He did not seem to be equipped for high altitudes, Hutchinson thought, but you never knew; he might well propose to hang about in the region of the mountain for the entire expedition. What was more, in Katmandu itself a news agency and a newspaper had each set up observation posts to pick up what they could of the news seeping back from the mountain. A room in the government guest-house had a bold notice pinned to its door: 'Keep Out: Monitoring in Progress'. This was the ad hoc office of a respectable Fleet Street newspaper which had reasonably assumed that the news from Everest would be coming back to Katmandu by wireless; with a powerful receiver it was planned to intercept such messages and also (it was whispered) to listen in to the cables being radioed down to India by the cable authorities. A big news agency had done the same thing. All kinds of odd journalists were arriving in Katmandu like converging scavengers, to pick up what they could, using

17

their claws if need be. Who knew how far they would travel into the mountains? You can place a copyright on dispatches, but there is no copyright on news. If a reporter could describe the expedition's departure from Katmandu, he might just as well describe its activities on the mountain (if he was determined enough to get there).

But Hutchinson had one heartening piece of news. He had established happy relations with the British Embassy, which lived then in an ugly house in a glorious garden and was still known to all the Nepalese as 'The Lines', in memory of the days when a British resident had a troop of Indian cavalry to protect him. The resident had evolved, under the inexorable pressures of history, into an ambassador, in the person of Mr. Christopher Summerhayes. Summerhayes was naturally doing all he could to help the Everest expedition, and he had promised Hutchinson that when a final message came from the mountain, announcing either success or failure, he would transmit it over his Foreign Office radio transmitter to London. This would, for that one message, obviate the delays and dangers of the cable office, and take the final news to London in a matter of moments. It was not a favour exclusively for *The Times*. If any other paper managed to secure the news first, the ambassador would undoubtedly perform the same service for it, his motive being not to take sides in a newspaper war, but simply to get the news from Everest home to England as quickly as possible.

It was on the veranda of the embassy that our caravan was assembled. By some dismal aberration in the Indian independence agreement, it later turned out that this building was now the property of the Indian government, and the British, who had built it, planted its gardens, and kept it spick and span through the years, had to move to a smaller place down the road; but in 1953 it still flew the Union Jack, and as one worked among the lawns and flowers, with the scent of blossoms heavy in the air, there frequently emerged from the interior of the building coveys of gentle servants bearing cool drinks. In such idyllic circumstances my own contribution to the work was chiefly advisory; but Roberts, who had arrived in Katmandu a few days before me, was very active checking loads, recruiting porters, ordering supplies. He was a Gurkha officer who looked like a witty bear, and he had been on several previous expeditions to the Himalaya. He believed whole-heartedly in living off the country, and was an authority on *chang*, the glutinous substance used by the Nepalese for beer, and on *rakhsi*, the methylated spirits with which they foster the wild illusion that they are drinking gin. Roberts was on leave from his regiment in Malaya, and had volunteered to convey to the expedition a large number of oxygen cylinders which had been flown into Katmandu too late to be taken by the main convoy.

He sat on the veranda surrounded by porters and bits of string. The coolies, 200 of them, had been recruited with government help and were now being organized, in a general sort of way, by a couple of foremen, one of them wearing round, goggle-like spectacles and carrying a lantern. The porters were dressed in rags, with funny peaked hats on their heads, and talked incessantly, now and then breaking into a few snatches of abuse. It had been decided how much each should carry, and as soon as the loads were experimentally distributed each man pottered off to rearrange the packages in the most comfortable way, tying boxes on top of one another, shifting the balance of weight, and adjusting the dirty headbands with which they bore a good deal of the burden. Hovering around the edges of this collection were some of the expedition's high-altitude porters, men of a very different breed. These were Sherpas, members of the Tibetan race which lives in the Everest region and which has for generations provided porterage for Himalayan expeditions. Their faces were brown and Mongolian, their bodies inexpressibly tough, their eyes bright, their movements jerky and decisive. They were all well-known climbing porters, who had forsaken their high native valleys to live in Darjeeling, in India, where they could more easily find work; they wore European clothing, and had a ready grasp of European needs and tastes.

Most of them were young and fit, recruited especially to climb high on Everest. One was rather different. He had come along to act as Roberts's personal Sherpa during the solitary climbs that officer proposed to do when he had delivered the oxygen. Long, long before this man had made his mark with British climbers, partly because of his excellent qualities, chiefly because of his extraordinary clothes. He had most lively tastes. In 1935, when he had first turned up with an expedition, he had been equipped with windproofs, snow-goggles, Balaclava, and the rest; and took to them so affectionately that for many weeks, in the hottest days of July and August, he would be seen dressed in the complete equipment of a mountaineer about to make a desperate assault upon some unassailable peak. In 1937, when he was in the Himalaya again, he wore a grey summer suit with thick white stockings worn outside his trousers. In 1949 those who encountered him in the hills reported a pair of sagging cotton shorts and a long-sleeved jerkin, from beneath which a few inches of portly figure protruded, and above which there dangled the coloured beads of an amulet. This year his appearance was no less distinctive. On his head was a brown woollen Balaclava helmet with a peak, like the hats the Russian Army used to wear. His grey sports shirt had polished major's crowns on its epaulettes. Over long woollen pants he wore a voluminous pair of blue shorts, and on his feet were elderly gym shoes. A confused variety of beads, tokens, and Tibetan charms dangled around his neck, and a bracelet hung upon his wrist. In one hand he flourished an iceaxe, in the other a fly-whisk. It was not for nothing that Sen

Tenzing, in the old days of gentlemanly climbing, had been christened by his British employers 'The Foreign Sportsman'.

Our party had responsibility for 60 crates of oxygen, all handsomely packed, and stamped in large letters: 'Dangerous: This Way Up'. On the cool veranda we checked the crates against the expedition's inventory, a list as long as a novel. Each had to be weighed and weighed again, in case the coolies, turning nasty on the road, decided that their burdens were excessive. The accepted load was sixty pounds (which I used to measure mentally in terms of pots of marmalade) and the accepted fee about £4 10 s. for the fortnight which the porters would spend on the road. A few years before this would have been considered excessive; but a constant stream of expeditions was passing through Nepal, not all of them bound by very stringent financial disciplines, and the porters now found themselves masters of a sellers' market. Poor things, with their bare corny feet and their spindly bodies, and the meagre pleasures of their lives, it would be hard to begrudge them a little extra money, however maddening the vagaries of their behaviour.

There were a few things to buy in the bazaar too: rice, flour and paraffin, candles and cotton thread. I bought some American tinned fruit, which looked delicious on the fading paper wrappings, but which had gone bad many long years before. I also acquired a handsome hurricane lamp, made in Czechoslovakia, by the light of which I proposed to read the *Oxford Book of Greek Verse* in the authentic manner of the scholar-mountaineer. It was odd buying things in Katmandu, for there was a perplexing sales-resistance on the part not of the consumer, but the shopkeeper. If you asked for an electric kettle you would be met by a blank if not hostile stare from a recumbent merchant; and if you managed to get hold of one, by forcing your way into the shop and breaking into a cupboard, you would have extreme difficulty in paying for it. I enjoyed this; for there was something about the veiled reluctance of the shopkeepers, and their persistence in guarding their merchandise, that seemed reminiscent of Katmandu in its palmy days, isolated behind its barrier of mountains, lonely and introspective, and occasionally invigorated by some appalling massacre (like the one when Queen Kot threw fifty of her courtiers down a well in the palace courtyard). The merchants were partly apathetic, but partly suspicious; and on the whole they preferred to have as little as possible to do with you, in case you reported them to the hangman. Katmandu was still a secretive city in 1953. There was a curfew at night, with passwords passed from hand to hand on grubby pieces of paper, by the light of flickering lamps; and the shopkeepers' eyes, I fancied, were deep with the reflections of conspiracy.

Slowly, despite the complexity of life in this peculiar place, our preparations were completed. Hutchinson had already made his mark with the cable authorities, and our first messages were reaching London quickly enough. There was of course no news from the expedition itself, out in the hinterland. Until the first of the mail runners came back, we were totally cut off from Hunt, so far as we knew; it would take ten days for a man from Katmandu to catch him up, and almost as long for one of his men to get back to us. The climbers, indeed, were out in a void, with Izzard hot on their heels. I spent my evenings studying the map. On its shiny surface (it was a photostat) I traced the course of our journey: by truck for a few miles to the edge of the valley of Katmandu, where the road ended, and thence by foot over the hills. If I had opportunity I would send back some dispatches during the march; otherwise I would begin my messages when I reached Sola Khumbu, the high alpine region around Everest where the Sherpas lived. In the meantime, no doubt, Izzard would be sending home good exclusive dispatches: but it was the end of the expedition rather than the beginning that was important to us, and that would not be for two months or more.

During these months my runners would be constantly on the move between Everest and Katmandu, carrying reports of progress on the mountain. This would certainly be expensive. At the bank in Katmandu, heavily guarded and run by an enthusiastic philatelist, I collected the money sent there by banker's order from London. It was several hundred pounds, and I had been assured that nobody in the region of Everest was interested in anything but good hard coin.

'No paper money for those boys,' said the experts. 'They might accept barter—say ten pounds of *tsampa* for a single journey, or five yards of woollen cloth—but you'd much better pay them in coin.'

This jungly advice I foolishly accepted. Many were the tedious hours I spent at the bank, counting out the money, so that my fingers were black from the coated filth upon it, like a bus conductor's at the end of the day; and when eventually we moved into the hills, two porters had to be paid just to carry the cash to pay the others with, a system which surely violates some fundamental economic law. When we got to Everest, of course, we found that the good Sherpas were just as happy with a ten-rupee note as they were with a coin; and I was needlessly condemned to stand watch over two tin boxes of treasure, heavily padlocked and sealed, the sort of thing you find in sunken galleons.

One fine morning at the end of March we discovered that all was ready, and loading our baggage into trucks we set off through the valley to the neighbouring town of Bhatgaon, which Roberts said was the end of the road. There we would rejoin our porters, and they would reassume their loads for the march. The valley of Katmandu was full of splendid medieval monuments, but there was nowhere quite so remarkable as Bhatgaon, which lies about twelve miles to the east of the capital. It was a town of dark and glowering appearance, instinct with the spirit of the Middle Ages. Its streets were narrow and tortuous, and in them you might well expect to meet the funeral procession of a plague, or mingle with branded slaves, or come across some defiant heretic blazing at the stake. Tall buildings with protruding cornices shaded these narrow passage-ways, and here and there were pools of muddy water, dark courtyards, and suggestive flights of steps. The doorways and lintels of this shadowy place were decorated with countless mythical images—rats and bears and monkeys, legendary giants, flowers, cabalistic symbols, wrestlers, kings, and gods; and the central square, suddenly flooded with sunlight, was surrounded by a splendid series of temple pagodas. What a marvellous and magnificent city to find deposited among the mountains! The Temple of the Five Stages at Bhatgaon is a culminating glory of Nepal's famous past, when the state was ruled by the Newar kings of old. It rises high and confident above the square, and the steep stone staircase leading to its entrance is guarded by an imposing series of figures. First, squatting at ease at the lowest level, is a giant with drooping black moustaches, carrying a huge club and shield, his great toes splayed out on the pedestal beside him. Next is a splendid elephant, chained and caparisoned. On the third level sits a dragon, baring his teeth in an ominous grin, as if he is about to pounce. On the fourth stands a prim and pompous eagle. High on the topmost level, beside the door of the temple, sits a terrible god, with six arms, a face like a frog's, a magnificent head-dress, and two glazed unrelenting eyes. Small boys and old men clamber about these figures, or sleep among their multitudinous limbs; but their total effect is one of awful reproach or warning, as if a whole bench of Judge Jeffreys has been frozen in the moment of sentence.

On a green field outside this memorable town our company assembled. It was really a parade ground of the Nepalese Army, and numbers of officers and soldiers watched us as we gathered there. The grass was very green, the sky very blue; hazy hills surrounded us on all sides, some of them thickly wooded, and if you looked hard to the north you could imagine the superb snow peaks which stood shimmering beyond. Nearby there was a pool, beautifully flagged with mellowed stones, and in it an old sage with a white beard washed his shirt unconcernedly. Coveys of small children wandered drooling through our caravan, grubbier and more persistent than an English mother could conceive in her most desolate nightmare.

By now we had about seventy Nepalese coolies, seven of them employees of mine. In Katmandu, jumbled and jostling among the congestions of the city, they had looked a ragged army indeed; but here in the open, as they manfully lifted their loads and prepared to move, they acquired a certain gnome-like dignity. Off they set through the streets of Bhatgaon, most of them stopping almost at once for a last good-bye, a farewell onion, or a pre-mature breather. Their silhouettes were strange as they stood on the ridge above the town; some had huge square boxes strapped to their backs, but some were crookedly loaded with baskets or boots, long protruding wireless aerials, lanterns, bundles of rags, or frying-pans. Some of this stuff was mine; most was the expedition's; and a little the porters took themselves, to relieve the hardships of the march to the mountain and enliven the long, leisurely orgy into which, I suspected, the empty march back again was to degenerate. By midmorning we were off, to a metaphorical flourish of trumpets and a few rather hopeless cries of 'Baksheesh!', swinging away down the valley tracks in fine form. That night, we said, we would camp at Banepa, on the edge of the valley, and next morning we would be in the hills.

But it was not to be; for later that day a queer thing happened. In the heat of the early afternoon Roberts and I, having searched without success for a beer-shop or a tea-house, settled down beside a stream for a drink and a sandwich. The setting was something short of Elysian, for it was a dusty, rocky hillside without much shade; and the stream, though it bubbled pleasantly, seemed to me to come almost directly from the outhouses of some huts on the hill above us. Nevertheless, we sat there comfortably, and ate our meal. It was not long, alas, before we were disturbed. A huge cloud of dust approached us along the track, and from it there gradually emerged a shootingbrake, bouncing and jolting and squeaking along the rough surface. *Good heavens!* was my first thought. *We could have driven here all the time!* But before I had time to reproach Roberts, who had been inspired by the need to toughen us all up as soon as possible, there stepped from the car Colonel Proud of the British Embassy, with a look of concern on his face.

A message had come from Hunt, he said, to say that many of the oxygen cylinders taken by the expedition proper were found to be deficient in pressure. Some of them were useless. Would we please check all the cylinders we had with us, to make sure they were not faulty too? This was serious. If they were leaking it might well mean the cancellation of the whole expedition. It would be almost impossible to fly out further supplies before the end of the Everest climbing season, and unless they wanted to make an attempt without oxygen the climbers would probably have to beat a dispiriting retreat.

Roberts decided to move on to Banepa, camp there for the night, and spend the next day checking the cylinders. It would mean opening sixty well-packed crates, inspecting their pressure gauges, and packing them up again; no simple task with little of the necessary equipment and only a rudimentary knowledge of the dangers of the danger of high-pressure oxygen. Proud ushered us into the car and bounded us eastward along the track, overtaking a few toiling coolies, skidding through a number of hamlets, until we could see the houses of Banepa in front of us. As we approached, it occurred to me to wonder how Hunt's message had reached Katmandu so swiftly. It was March 31, and the climbers had probably just assembled in the area of Namche Bazar, the headquarters village of the Sherpas. *For that matter,* I suddenly thought, jerking myself upright in my seat, *how did the message reach Katmandu at all?* No runner could have come all the way from Namche— 170 miles or more—in three or four days. The village was in almost virgin country, first visited by Europeans only four years before, remote and shuttered. What on earth had happened? Had we overlooked some crucial factor in planning the news from Everest?

'By the way, Colonel,' I said as casually as I could, for I hated to bore people with my private anxieties. 'How did the message from Hunt reach you so quickly?'

Proud was doing something to the lens hood of his camera, but looked up with a smile and said mildly:

'Oh by radio, you know. It seems there's some kind of a radio station at Namche Bazar!'

A radio at Namche, almost within sight of the mountain! With a great crackling of wrappers and silver paper, I helped myself to a humbug.

3

Travelling

WE CAMPED on a green plateau above the village of Banepa, and set about opening all the cases. It was a mucky village, all dirty inquisitive people and flyblown stalls of vegetables, but the high ground above it was cool and pleasant. The *chang* was excellent, not thick as it is in the higher country, but as thin as pale cider and with rather the same taste. Only a few idlers wandered up to watch us; the main body of the expedition had passed this way, and we were a much less imposing sight. Two Buddhist priests strolled over from a neighbouring temple, dressed in their vivid saffron robes, very young but dignified. One or two persistent beggar girls whined their way through the baggage, impervious to invective; and some of the more horrible urchins of Bhatgaon seemed to have followed us all the way to Banepa. Nevertheless we managed well enough. Soon we found that by prising open one edge of a crate you could peer inside and see the pressure gauge; and by noon on the following day we had done this to all of them and packed them up again. The results were reassuring. Of the 111 cylinders, only 11 were deficient. The expedition could proceed. We handed a report to Colonel Proud, and soon after lunch set off again in majesty into the hills.

I was much preoccupied with the problems of the wireless transmitter. It was apparently operated by the Indian government, for Hunt's message had reached Proud through the medium of the Indian Embassy in Katmandu. The Indians had inherited from the British their old nebulous hegemony over Nepal, and they were of course concerned for the security of her northern frontiers, particularly the passes through the Himalaya which formed gateways into India. But it was extraordinary that there should be a radio station so deep in the wilds, and in a region so secluded, It alarmed me to think what the presence of this phenomenon might mean. Hunt had obviously established friendly relations with its operators; but supposing Izzard or some other roaming correspondent managed to persuade them to transmit messages only for him, to the exclusion of *The Times?* It would not matter how high I climbed up the mountain, as the expedition's accredited correspondent. Namche was only thirty miles from Everest, and the news of any great event on the mountain would certainly seep through there, by the Sherpa grapevine, long before I could get a runner back to Katmandu. It was a disagreeable prospect; who knew, perhaps Izzard already had the transmitter firmly in his grasp, and was happily sending messages back over the air?

But there was no point in fretting, and since the Everest country was as remote and unimaginable to me as the mountains of the moon, I could not clearly envisage any situation there. Instead I devoted myself to the pleasures of the march, which has since become, thanks to the labours of innumerable chroniclers, one of the best-known nature rambles in the world. Ours was a pleasant, leisurely walk. It was the custom of the climbers to begin the march early, and only settle down for breakfast after two or three hours' marching. Our way was very different. Long after the sun was beating down on our tents pale hands could be seen groping between the tent-flaps; and into them, in a trice, the Sherpas would thrust steaming mugs of tea. Roberts was usually soon outside, checking a load or quelling an incipient mutiny; but my progress into the open air was slow indeed, and agreeable. Gradually I would emerge into the sunshine, to sit on the portals of my tent and clean my teeth, and smell the clean hill air, and listen to the distant sizzling of breakfast. Soon a company of local yokels would gather round to share my pleasure, and we would exchange a few ineffective words of greeting. I had a small radio receiver with me, and before long I would tune it in to London for the news; but generally I had only time to hear of a minor disaster or two, to the incredulous hilarity of the Nepalese, before Sen Tenzing would come rolling up the hillside to tell me that breakfast was ready, sahib, and could he now demolish the tent?

A delightful way to start the day! There was scrambled egg, and tea, and *chupattis* with Cooper's marmalade, even sometimes bread, for my wife had bought two tins of yeast from the Army and Navy, which gave us a great advantage over other travellers in the Himalaya that season. As we munched, the first of our porters, anxious to finish the day early, would set off along the track in the direction of our next camping site. Harrying their flanks were the two overseers; one still wearing his spectacles and brandishing his lantern, smudged with smoke; the other equipped with a big black umbrella. Their force was certainly varied. Some of the porters were old and grizzled, their shanks withered, their fingers long and bony; some were young and incorrigibly cheerful, always wandering off the route to find some drink or flirt with the local houris. They were all men from the valley, and as the track climbed higher into the hills they lost some of their vigour and good humor, and began behaving with a certain trade-union waywardness; but at the beginning they were willing enough, and waved us good morning as we scraped up the last traces of our scrambled egg.

No ethereal beauty haunted these foothills. They were dusty, brown, and drab; the villages sordid and mean, the people terribly poor. Heat shimmered along the track, and at every fountain (gushing from antique iron lions' mouths beside the way) you were tempted to stop and drink. All in all, I did not much like this region; but Roberts was a Gurkha officer, and most of his gallant men had come from Nepal. He was at pains to assure me that the weedy and cross-eyed young men we encountered in the villages were not altogether typical of his soldiers.

'Ah yes, but these are the Hindings! They're *quite* different. Our men come from the Bindung country—over the hill there—*altogether* different. These people have intermarried with the Pontungs. Wait till you see the Bindungs!'

But no, over the hill the Bindungs seemed as cross-eyed as ever, and before long Roberts was reduced to suggesting that his men came from that country up there, beyond the ridge, pointing to a place so hideously inaccessible that there was no possibility of my ever penetrating to it.

So the days passed happily as we trudged along the tracks, sometimes dozing in the sunshine, sometimes pausing for lunch beside some limpid rivulet. In these foothills there were always interesting sounds to hear. Innumerable ridiculous birds sang the hours away, among them a cuckoo so indefatigable that its thick cry echoed from every hill, very loud and energetic. In the villages there were always drums beating and weird stringed instruments playing rhythmically. In our little camp the porters' child-like chatter competed with the deep bass crooning of Sen Tenzing, alleged to be the music of his devotions. Often the still was shattered by the distant rasping of cross women's voices, or the clucking of chickens; at night a hyena sometimes howled out of the darkness.

Why the inhabitants thought we were travelling that way, loaded with such queer implements, I have no idea. Even the porters were vague, I think, about the eventual purposes of their labours; and the villagers in general seemed to accept us merely as quaint animals passing by, on a migration perhaps. Sometimes, though, a sage would detect ulterior motives. In particular, such silly old men were always anxious to look through our binoculars, almost invariably through the wrong end.

'Why are you so interested in these things?' we asked one man. 'All they do is magnify, just like a pair of spectacles. Look at this typewriter, now—it will write a letter for me, more clearly than the finest scribe. This camera will make an image of you in a trice, for me to take home in my pocket and keep forever. This small bottle of pills will clear away my headache. This little radio box will bring me voices from places a year's march away. Why do you always pick upon the binoculars?'

'Aha, sahib!' the sage replied slyly. 'I know better than that! I am not so simple! I know that through these miraculous glasses you can see under the surface of the earth, so that you know where the gold lies, and the diamonds, and all the other treasures of the mountains! One more look, sahib, I beg you, through the miraculous glasses!'

They were a peaceable people, the Nepalese of the foothills, who would never dream of harming you; and during my entire stay in Nepal nothing was stolen from me. But they gave themselves a threatening air by carrying at all times the famous Gurkha dagger called the *kukri*. It was a curved and murderous instrument, worn prominently in the waistband, and chiefly used for cutting meat, chopping wood, opening tins, and other such mild activities. Almost every male carried one, and the little Nepalese, who wore nothing much but a hat and a jerkin, were sometimes all but dwarfed by the huge knife strapped firmly to their stomachs.

The women, though unarmed, sometimes managed neverthe-less to look more ferocious. With their matted hair and low brows, their tattered dark dresses and their bangles, they sat like witches over the big pots in which they brewed their *chang*, pouring the coagulated liquid from one receptacle to another, stirring and filtering it with sticks or their dirty fingers, some-times breaking into raucous laughter, and finally thrusting a pan of the drink viciously in the direction of the passing sahib. I was generally much too alarmed by these wild ladies to refuse the stuff, however thick and sticky its consistency, and whatev-er the conditions of its brewing. Sometimes I remembered that I had not been inoculated very thoroughly against Eastern dis-eases; but I reminded myself, as I masticated the brew, of Lord Fisher's favourite dictum: 'Do right, and damn the odds!'

These hill villages were busy places. A constant stream of foot traffic passed through them, taking produce to Katmandu. Every day we met convoys of half-naked porters, loaded high. They passed us silently, moving deliberately, smelling of sweat and dirt. Often they carried vast quantities of onions, with the green leaves still on them; sometimes they had wicker cages of small chickens, with roosters tied by the leg to the topmost cages and flapping their wings impotently. The porters carried only blankets, cooking pots, and a few minor implements for themselves; at night they bought their food locally, cooked it over an open fire, and rolled up in their ragged bed-clothes beneath a rock or in a gulley. It was a hard life. Their bodies were riddled with disease, and for most of the year they were out on the hill tracks, away from their wives and families.

One morning, a few days out of Katmandu, I met a group of such men travelling in the direction of the capital without any loads. They at once stopped and greeted me, and turned out to be the first of Hunt's returning porters, who had taken their loads to Sola Khumbu and were now journeying home. All was going well, they said. The expedition was safely in the Sherpa country, and Mr. Izzard, they were happy to be able to tell me, was somewhere in the region of Namche Bazar. I asked them to wait for a moment, and sitting down beside the track wrote a short dispatch describing our progress and reporting the ubiquity of the cuckoos: this I gave them, together with a letter to Hutchinson, and they delivered it safely.

Our progress was not very swift, but was steady enough. The heat was intense, and the flies trying. Sometimes gigantic beautiful butterflies floated past us; sometimes a malicious buzzing heralded the arrival of an enormous flying beetle, large enough to make you duck and shield your head. Often we stopped for a swim in some clear swift stream running down from the mountains, or climbed a neighbouring eminence to catch a glimpse of the distant snow peaks through the obscuring haze.

So we reached the big bazaar village of Meksin, the half-way mark, and felt ourselves approaching Everest. (On the map this place was bafflingly called Those, a name which seemed to mean absolutely nothing to its inhabitants; but poor map, it proved to be so hopelessly inaccurate throughout the journey that I grew quite sorry for it.) We approached the village down a beautiful narrow valley, thickly wooded and watered by a delectable rushing stream, a first hint of the alpine country that was to come. Meksin itself, though, was still a village of the foothills. It had a wide market street, thronged with idlers and lethargic merchants, and a few open shops where you could buy such luxuries as lampglasses and mirrors. On the outskirts there were one or two fine old houses, in the manner of the Newar architects, one of them looking strangely like an English coaching inn, so that as I passed I half-expected to hear fruity English voices from the taproom, or smell the Brussels sprouts. They do some iron smelting at Meksin, and through the open door of another building we glimpsed the glare of furnaces and the strong bared muscles of the iron men.

We camped on a wide grassy space outside the town, on the banks of a river; and that night I typed out a second dispatch. 'Summon me,' said I to the watching crowd, 'summon me a runner!' A runner appeared at once, miraculously, and named his price. I sealed my package, paid him half the fee, and instructed him to collect the other half when he arrived at 'The Lines'; and that same evening, before the sun went down, I saw him stride off into the gorge that led to the west.

Our own way led firmly into the east, into mountain country, staunchly Buddhist, strongly Tibetan in flavour. The woods and thickets we passed through now were gorgeous with rhododendrons and magnolia; the air was sharp, and the grass of the high meadows deliciously green. One afternoon I was stumbling down a rocky track in a thick wood when I heard a sharp chattering, and the sound of footfalls approaching me through the trees. What's this? I thought, for there was something odd and pungent about the noises. Goblins? Dwarfs? People who live in the trees? A moment later, and they appeared around a corner, four men and three women. They were small brown beings with gleaming faces, talking and laughing very quickly, with great animation of expression. The men wore brown woollen cloaks, slung around their waists like bath towels, and embroidered woollen boots; the women, their skirts tucked up to their knees, had pretty coloured aprons and little linen hats. All seven carried on their backs huge bundles of indefinable matter, closely strapped and packaged. These strange folk were moving through the wood with an almost unearthly speed and vigour, dancing up the track with a gay sprightly movement, like fauna or leprechauns, still chattering and laughing as they went. They smiled at me as they passed, white teeth gleaming beneath almond eyes; and as they swept away up the hill I knew we had entered the country of the Sherpas.

Soon the symbols of Tibetan Buddhism were all around us. The mystical slogan of the faith, *Om Mane Padme Hun!* (Hail to the Jewel in the Lotus Leaf!) appeared on walls and shrines in Tibetan characters. Tall white prayer flags flapped in the breeze from their poles, and at every pass the pious had affixed small fluttering pieces of fabric to trees or sticks in gratitude to the divinities. Here and there were prayer wheels, rotating drums inscribed with prayers which could be turned by an indolent flick of the hand from the faithful. Several times we stopped at monasteries, and were greeted by kindly monks with greasy butter tea. I remember well the serene face of the Abbot of Risingo, who walked out to our camp with his two little dogs playing about his heels; a crowd of his congregation jostled about him, eager to touch his clothes or kiss his hand, and he talked paternally to each one. The villages were more spacious now, the houses well built and inviting; and though we were among devout Buddhists the villagers readily sold us tough and scraggy chickens for dinner, only stipulating that we must wring their necks ourselves.

We were still alternately climbing hills and slithering into deep valleys; but gradually the altitude was increasing, and one morning I walked around a grassy slope, in lovely open country, and suddenly saw in front of me a dazzling panorama of the snow peaks. It was the most wonderful sight I had ever seen. The mountains stretched from one end of my horizon to the other, some of them streaked with shadow, some ineffably clean and sparkling. They were as cool, still, and silent as figures of Greek sculpture, but they looked strangely friendly, too, for all their majesty. I very much liked the look of these marvellous things.

Presently the track, crossing a high mountain range, tumbled helter-skelter down into a valley, and at the bottom we found the rushing stream of the Dudh Khosi. This river flows southwards from the Everest region into India; I looked at it with interest, for it was on these turbulent waters that I was supposed to float my watertight dispatches to that unhappy colleague at Jogbani. There was a rickety bridge made of motley poles and branches, across which we cautiously crept; and on the other side we found ourselves in a beautiful green valley of enchantment, fragrant with pine leaves, with the tumbling water shining beside our path. There were wide meadows to camp upon, and always above our heads, peeping through gulleys, suddenly standing sentinel at the heads of passes, were the snow peaks, now very close.

This was Sola Khumbu, the central province of the Sherpas. At each hamlet the inhabitants turned out with bowls of *chang* or mugs of *rakhsi,* and our own Westernized Sherpas got steadily drunker as we advanced. For long hours they would sit upon the terrace of some friendly house, drinking and laughing boisterously, only bestirring themselves towards the end of the day in time to catch up the caravan, erect the tents, and prepare the camp. The youngest of the three, Ang Nyima, was the most difficult of them. He would stagger into camp with a foolish grin on his face and a cigarette hanging from his lips, looking more like a London street hawker, selling sub-standard nylons, than a Himalayan climber; but there was a sense of fun about him, all the same, that I sometimes found obscurely agreeable, and a feeling of latent strength and energy, as if he were only sowing a few preliminary wild oats before the job began.

We were now only two days from Hunt's rear base, established at the Buddhist monastery of Thyangboche, south of Everest. As we were late Roberts decided to push on with part of the caravan to deliver some of the oxygen. I was to usher in the rest. Accordingly I was alone when, the following morning, I walked around a corner in the track, in a lonely and exquisitely beautiful part of the valley, and found myself face to face with a European coming the other way. I instantly recognized him. Ralph Izzard and I had first met in Egypt some years before; but he had forgotten the occasion, and since it had never been made public that a correspondent would be accredited to the expedition, he now thought that I was one of the climbers. He was an imperturbable soul, and said 'Good morning!' rather as if we were meeting in the underground on the way to Blackfriars.

'Good morning!' I said. 'Nice to see you!'

'Have a cup of tea,' said he, 'and a bun.'

So we sat down upon a rock, and his excellent cook provided a pot of tea and some cakes. It was a curious encounter. His bold journey had surprised the climbers, who had scarcely expected to find a *Daily Mail* correspondent wandering unattached around the glaciers, but had not broken their nerve. Faithful to their contract with *The Times*, they had given him very little information, and he had been chiefly restricted to descriptions of the scene, accounts of his own experiences, and whatever he could actually see of the climbers' activities. He had climbed to the very foot of Everest, up the Khumbu Glacier, and although the movement on to the mountain had not yet begun, was now on his way back to Katmandu. I found this decidedly suspect; and since he was as keen to know of Hunt's plans as I was to know of his, we settled down happily to pump each other. He was understandably reticent. Yes, he was going back to Katmandu. For good? He wasn't sure. He had to go down to Calcutta, for one thing and another, and then—perhaps back to Nepal? It depended partly upon his newspaper. He had been in the Himalaya before, and did not want to renew his acquaintance with the leeches of the monsoon. But there, one could only wait and see.

What about me, now? He didn't suppose I could say much, in view of our contractual obligations, but would I mind if he took my photograph, at least?

'Oh by all means,' I said, throwing out my chest like an open-circuit man, and jutting my black beard into the breeze, 'fire away!'

But it never appeared in the *Daily Mail*, for my resolution failed me and I told him the truth. I was no mountaineer, but a reporter like himself. We had several more cups of tea on the strength of it, discussed at length the affairs of newspapers, and parted. When I looked around, from an eminence higher on the track, I could see his long lop-sided figure striding away through the pine trees.

I had not dared to mention the Namche transmitter, in case he had not come across it; and he would obviously not mention it to me. I had a horrible feeling that he had arranged matters satisfactorily with the radio people, and was now going back to India to collect new equipment during the opening stages of the climb; returning to Everest to scoop the world when somebody reached the summit. The idea haunted me as we marched, and now that I had seen the country I knew how easily a fit man could settle down among these people for a few months, waiting only to seize upon a Sherpa coming down from the mountain to extract the great news from him and send it winging home.

Before long I reached Namche myself. The track up the valley suddenly climbed a steep hill, thickly covered with pines and junipers, with the sound of the rushing water far away through the trees. At the top of it was the village, set in a bowl of the mountains, with a background of snow peaks. It was built like an amphitheatre, thirty or forty stout little houses erected in a cirque, all facing down the hill, as if they expected to see some kind of performance in the open ground at the bottom. The altitude was about 9,000 feet, but the village looked a cosy and comfortable place, with its heavy wooden doors and crooked lanes. Namche Bazar is the capital of the Sherpas. Many are the celebrated mountain porters who have come from this place or from neighbouring villages; and as I walked into it I noticed several brown and smiling men wearing odd bits of mountain clothing—windproofs, Swiss boots, and big quilted jackets.

'Good day, Mr. Morris, Major Roberts told us to expect you!' said a voice. I looked around to see an enormous bearded Sikh, in some sort of uniform topped by a fur-lined jacket. 'Please! Come this way, Mr. Tiwari would like to see you.' He led the way, at a spanking pace, off the track and through a number of backyards; up and down the various strata of construction that seem to characterize the outskirts of Sherpa villages; round and about low walls, in and out of little alleys; until we arrived at a large, low wooden building with two or three Indians, in different stages of uniform, chatting outside it. We entered and climbed a flight of stairs, and there in the dark recesses of an upstairs room was the wireless transmitter. It looked quite a powerful one, and near it was a contraption like a stationary bicycle used to generate its electric power.

Mr. Tiwari was the Indian police officer in charge of this small but significant post. He was a stocky man muffled in thick clothes, and greeted me affably; stumping about the room and shouting instructions through the window and down the stairs, he soon organized a cup of tea and a tray of miscellaneous delicacies. Sure enough, Hunt's message about the oxygen had come over his radio, for he had been told by the Indian Embassy in Katmandu to transmit any urgent messages for the expedition. He talked to Katmandu, as I remember, twice a day. 'What on earth do you find to talk about?' I inquired, but he was not anxious to discuss these things, In fact, this strange little unit was placed there to keep an eye on the traffic that crossed into Nepal from Tibet. Namche was not far from the Nangpa La, the chief gateway into eastern Nepal from the north. A constant stream of traffic crosses this 19,000-foot pass, the yak caravans carrying rice and vegetables north into Tibet and salt south into Nepal. There was little doubt in 1953 that Communist agents were using this difficult route to enter Nepal, and thence India; and the Delhi government was understandably anxious, under the terms of its agreement with Nepal, to keep some check on their movements. Occasionally Indian aircraft flew overhead, presumably on photo-reconnaissances (and once during the expedition an aircraft that looked like a Spitfire approached the region from the north). This was one of the ideological frontiers of the world. There were rumours that the Communists were building air bases on the high Tibetan plateau over the mountains; and this little radio station was a side show of the cold war.

Tiwari knew all about Izzard, but I could not make out if he had arranged to send any messages for him. He would, however, if I liked, transmit a short piece to Katmandu for me. It would go to the Indian Embassy, and they would pass it on to Mr. Summerhayes. I jumped at the offer, and hastily typed out a short dispatch. When, two days later, it appeared in the paper, a kindly sub-editor headed it with the dateline: 'Namche Bazar (by runner to Katmandu)': thus giving any competitors the salutary impression that our employees could run 170 miles in forty-eight hours. I thanked the Indians, we exchanged compliments, and I wandered off into the village to find somewhere to sleep.

I was perplexed by their attitude. Had they really made an arrangement with Izzard long before? I had emphasized the nature of my connexion with the expedition: but might they not be open to suggestion from any other correspondent who turned up in Namche when I was away on the mountain? Would any news I sent over the radio be available to all comers at the receiving end in Katmandu, thus ensuring that other newspapers got it before we did? Kind though Mr. Tiwari had been, in conversation with him I felt we were somehow sparring with each other; it might have been his police training; or he might, quite reasonably, suspect that I had come with some shady political motive. It was all very difficult, but the essence of the discovery was good: here within a few days' march of the mountain was an instrument that could get the news from Everest back to civilization in a matter of minutes, thus altering the whole complexion of my assignment. The problem now was to ensure that it got back safely and to the correct ultimate destination.

My camp bed had been set up on much the most public veranda in the whole village, on the terrace of a house kept by a hospitable old merchant. There another cup of tea was awaiting me, together with bowls of milky *chang* kindly contributed by my hosts. A large crowd of Sherpas stood around the perimeter of my sleeping quarters; in the front row hordes of children, pretty to look at despite their runny noses; behind, the serried ranks of adults, staring at me fixedly, occasionally swopping comments with their neighbours, responsive to my every smile and gesture; so that one could play upon their emotions like an actor with his audience, now elating them with an expression of appreciation, now intriguing them with a search for the tooth-brush, now convulsing them with a deft decomposition of the camp bed. Long after the evening was upon us they still stood there, and I could see the men at the back craning their necks for a better view; but gradually they dispersed, as the night came on, and I was left alone on my balcony with an old man with a white beard, wearing a high ornate fur-lined cap, who was burrowing and ferreting in the multitudinous bags of his luggage. The night was clear and frosty, and high above the village, all around us, stood the mountains.

As I lay on my back in the stillness, only disturbed by the unwrapping of cloths and the tearing of paper from the old man's corner, I worked out the problem of the transmitter. The first thing was that it was public, in the sense that nothing I sent over it would be confidential. I simply could not afford, however friendly Mr. Tiwari and his associates, to send some important piece of news over it 'in clear'; it was bound to leak out in Katmandu. Supposing I sent dispatches in code? It would be easy enough to do; the codes were in my pocket. But, I realized, Tiwari could scarcely agree to transmit something he did not understand himself. I noticed he had read my little dispatch that afternoon with some care, and I could not see him accepting mumbo-jumbo. Could I afford to give him a key to the codes, for his own private information? I thought of those keen and unscrupulous correspondents who might well penetrate to Namche during the coming months; I remembered Mr. Tiwari's professional duties, as a purveyor of information; and reluctantly decided I could not.

There was only one alternative, and I hope Tiwari has long ago forgiven me for resorting to it. I must produce another code in which messages enciphered *seemed* to be in clear. Such a message would make perfect sense—but it would be the wrong sense. This meant that for every word or phrase I wanted to encipher, I must devise a code phrase, so that several words run together would emerge as a sensible sentence. Because this would be rather a complicated system, and because I could obviously only use the thing once or twice, I decided that I must deny myself the use of the transmitter, however obliging the Indians, until the last crucial message of success or failure—and I assumed, under the pressure of some psychological compulsion, that success was all I need bother about. This was the code I compiled, allowing me simply to tell London that Everest had been climbed, and to name the members of the successful assault party:

Message to begin	:	*Snow Conditions Bad*
Band	:	*South Col Untenable*
Bourdillon	:	*Lhotse Face Impossible*
Evans	:	*Ridge Camp Untenable*
Gregory	:	*Withdrawal to West Basin*
Hillary	:	*Advanced Base Abandoned*
Hunt	:	*Camp Five Abandoned*
Lowe	:	*Camp Six Abandoned*
Noyce	:	*Camp Seven Abandoned*

Tenzing	:	*Awaiting Improvement*
Ward	:	*Further News Follows*
Westmacott	:	*Assault Postponed*
Wylie	:	*Weather Deteriorating*
Sherpa	:	*Awaiting Oxygen Supplies*
All Else Genuine		

I typed only three copies of this cipher. Two were for myself. The third I later sealed in innumerable containers and entrusted to the most reliable runner I could find; who, in the custom of his kind, took it back to Katmandu as swift as an eagle, and handed it safely to Hutchinson.

The old man was grunting in his shadows, and there was the clink of coin. I crossed the veranda to talk to him. He was surrounded by the wrappings of his baggage, and was now counting his money. Strange were the coins he was handling, inscribed with queer signs and letterings, and now and again he inspected a crinkly currency note, thick and heavily lettered, like an old parchment. This was Tibetan money, and on the following day the old man would be travelling with his little caravan of yaks, across the Nangpa I.a into that shadowy country.

'Come with me, sahib!' he said, leaning over his sacks and baggage. 'I will take you there tomorrow, and you can help me do my business. We will leave early, at dawn, and travel fast! Why go to the mountain? It is only a hardship. Come with me!'

But I refused, unable to explain to him why I might never come back again, and helped him to gather up his scattered possessions; and after sharing the last of the *rakhsi* in the bottom of my water-bottle, we parted and slept.

4

Arrival

HUNT'S REAR BASE CAMP at Thyangboche monastery was ten miles or so higher than Namche, and next morning I set off again to the north. If I had seen Everest during the march, I had been ignorant enough not to recognize it; but from the ridge directly above Namche it was unmistakable. There it stood, a great crooked cone of a thing, at once lumpish and angular. The vast rock wall of Nuptse obscured its haunches, and on either side, stretching away to the horizon, stood splendid snow peaks, rank upon rank. A plume of snow flew away from the summit of Everest, like a flaunted banner; in a setting so beautiful (diffused as the whole scene was by a gentle haze) it seemed to me that Chomolungma, as the Sherpas called our mountain, was awaiting our arrival with a certain sullen defiance.

Thyangboche lies at the top of a hill, overlooking the confluence of two streams, and the path up there becomes disagreeably steep. The altitude—about 12,500—was enough to affect the newcomer unaccustomed to such heights, and I found myself getting both breathless and disgruntled. Often I stopped among the groves of juniper for a mug of water and a meditation; and often cheerful Sherpas would come bounding down the path, staring at me curiously; but it seemed an awful long way up the hill. The poor porters from Katmandu also found it heavy going. This was about the limit of their altitude; they were valley men, who did not like travelling high. Some of them had deserted us already in the night, leaving their loads to be taken by eager Sherpa volunteers; the rest laboured on, breathing heavily, with occasional mutinous mutters.

But after an hour or two of climbing we emerged on the sparkling green plateau that crowned the hill; and there stood the monastery of Thyangboche. To the Buddhists of that region, it was a very sacred place. The monastery was equal in sanctity to the sister-house of Rongbuk, on the Tibetan side of Everest, and the site was preserved as a sanctuary, where no living thing might be harmed, even by the Sherpas (whose Buddhism is sometimes flexible). The monastery had rather a slatternly look about it, for the cluttered buildings that surrounded it were a little tumbledown, and the piles of stones that served to secure the roofs added to the feeling of incipient dereliction. But a fine knob of gold surmounted the central building, and in front of it were two noble *chortens,* or shrines, on the edge of the green. Meadows bright with primula stood all about this place, and the sides of its hill were thick with forests of larch, pine, and juniper. Musk-deer and pheasant wandered through the thickets. Overshadowing all this green preserve, and giving the scene drama as well as beauty, were the Himalayan peaks, like watchful gods.

A friendly monk in a russet robe drew me aside into one of the neighbouring buildings and plied me with brick tea and *rakhsi.* He had a delightful face, fat and impish, and he wrapped his dirty trappings about him with the air of a satyr recently emerged from a debauchery. We had no fluent language in common; but he chatted away volubly, with an appealing earnestness, and after a time it dawned on me that he had a characteristically ecclesiastical request to make: would I care to make a contribution towards the repair of the roof? I suspected there were few societies dedicated to the preservation of Thyangboche monastery, and there were certainly no archiepiscopal commissions to protect its rotting lintels; so I happily paid my share and presently, rolling a little, I think, from the *rakhsi,* he ushered me out into the meadows again.

There I had a second welcome. In an adjoining field I could see the tents of the expedition. There was a big yellow pyramid tent, a number of smaller ones, piles of miscellaneous equipment, the movement of Sherpas and porters, and a general sense of determined preparation, the whole very suitably surmounted by a large Union Jack. A rough rope fence had been placed around the camp to keep out those many Sherpas who stood transfixed to the spot like yokels at the County Show; and when I walked towards the entrance a man came out to meet me. He was a lithe and eager figure, moving briskly and gracefully, with plus fours and a wide felt hat. As he approached his brown face split into a dazzling smile, and he reached out a hand to welcome me. 'Good morning, sir,' he said. 'Welcome! I am Tenzing!'

I always remember with pleasure my first sight of this famous person, there in his own country, so keen and dashing and unspoilt, still a simple and uncluttered man despite the celebrity that was already accumulating about him. He was thirty-nine then, but looked less, and seemed the incarnation of healthy mountain living; indeed I always thought of him more as some splendid creature of the snows than as a member of our prosaic human species. This was not racial snobbery, as the Indian chauvinists would say; it was biological humility. So, feeling as though Oberon were leading me into the woods, I followed Tenzing into the camp, and joined the expedition.

Not everyone was there. The climbers had been doing their acclimatization trials, here and there in the surrounding mountains. One team, led by Edmund Hillary, was now making the first incursion into the icefall of Everest. Hunt himself was somewhere up the Khumbu Glacier, the harsh highway that connected Thyangboche with the foot of the mountain. Most of the others were in camp, testing their oxygen equipment, doing obscure things to bits of equipment, and talking a good deal about the doings of climbers, a subject which always seemed to get back, sooner or later, to something called 'the Climbers' Club Hut at Helyg'. I have often been asked, of course, what the members of the Everest expedition were *really* like, and have always felt anticlimactic in having to reply lamely that, well, they were all really jolly nice chaps, you know. But this I will allow myself to say; that after two or three months in their company, in the rigours of the scree or the dangers of the icefall, I developed a passionate dislike for the Climbers' Club Hut at Helyg. What bleak prospects of communal evenings stretch away from the name! How the conversation must bounce from Schools to the West Face of the Grymwych, and back to Schools again! How tiresome the noise of those elderly sports cars, how mournful the tea stirred with a bent spoon, or the warm beer drunk from the can! 'Ah!' they say. 'But you have to be a climber to *understand!*' If I were a climber, I would be a rich one, and stay at the best hotel, and be driven away to the rock-face, and return like the old heroes of Everest to chicken in aspic. The Climbers' Club Hut at Helyg! Grrr!

Do not let me give the impression that the evening at Thyangboche was in any way threadbare. On the contrary, it was luxurious. The big tent, in which I was given a corner, was warm and comfortable. The food was excellent, scrambled eggs and pudding. The fire blazed high with logs and sticks, incited by frequent blasts of oxygen from a convenient cylinder. The conversation ranged over a wide field. There were men of many kinds of knowledge in this party. It included soldiers, doctors, a brain surgeon, an agricultural statistician, a movie-photographer, the director of a travel agency, a geologist, two schoolmasters, an authority on guided missiles, a bee-keeper, and me. There was nothing we could not talk about. I remember distinctly conversations about the Plymouth Brethren, racing, philately, the cost of education, social development in the Navy, Liverpool, Edgar Allan Poe, and the Climbers' Club Hut at Helyg. If Wilfrid Noyce could speak with the elegance of a Charterhouse poet, Michael Westmacott could tell us how many cubic feet of turnips equalled a pound of average pig. I dare say there were moments of bickering among these men; if so, I either did not hear them or have forgotten them; and I only remember one moment of active disagreement. It was a team chosen not only for its climbing skill, but also for its ability for friendship; and as a passenger I can vouch for its kindliness.

Tenzing, whose limited English meant that he could not take his proper part in these conversations, had found a Sherpa servant to stay with me throughout the expedition. His name was Sonam, and he came from the village of Chaunrikharka, a few miles down the valley. He was a small, stocky man, mild-mannered and quiet-spoken, past the age for very high climbing, but a fast mover and a most willing worker. I lived in the closest association with him for the next three months, and never once had cause for complaint; and later I became his guest at his house. Sonam gathered around him a wild, smiling team of local Sherpas, their long hair braided behind their heads, their cloaks gathered about them purposefully. All the Nepalese porters had been paid off, and were on their way home. These tough Sherpas (and their wives) would therefore carry my baggage up the glacier to the foot of the mountain. Hunt had insisted that I must not depend on him for food and supplies; so I had to allow not only for my bags, but also for stacks of firewood which must be brought up from the tree line to the top of the glacier. My platoon also included six eager and athletic men, bright-eyed and supple, who had agreed to be my runners. I warned them that if the route to Katmandu proved unsatisfactory, they might have to travel through the Terai jungle to India. They demurred at this, complaining of robbers and wild animals and malaria. I gave them each a packet of anti-malarial tablets and an advance of pay, and they thereupon agreed, on condition that I did not send them that way unless I really had to. I never did. It was a splendid company, my band of Sherpas, untouched by any tarnish of civilization, honest and faithful always.

Charles Evans and Alfred Gregory were leaving the next morning for the mountain, and they suggested that I come with them. To be honest, I had rather looked forward to a few lazy days among the meadows. While I had always admired Mallory's famous reason for wanting to climb Everest, I was convinced that it would still be there next week; but I was ashamed to admit it, and accepted their invitation. We left early next morning, strolling through the delicious woods of Thyangboche among the lovely fresh smells of morning. The grassy path was flecked with blue primula; I picked one or two to send home to my wife. Now and then odd gurgles from the wood told of the presence of some crouching bird, and sometimes we caught glimpses of deer. Unlike the valley porters, my Sherpas moved at least as fast as I did. My gear was now reduced to essentials: a typewriter; a camp bed; a radio receiver; a walkie-talkie, with an aerial and tripod; my two pantechnicons of treasure; some books; lots of paper and carbon; a few cheap items of mountain equipment; and a couple of sleeping-bags. I wore my corduroy trousers throughout the expedition, and on my head I placed a soft felt hat, its shiny lining ripped out of it, which I had bought for a few rupees in Delhi. The day was fine, the climate delightful, and we walked through the woodlands merrily.

It was about 20 miles from Thyangboche to the foot of Everest and the first part of this journey lay through green country, the trees gradually thinning, the grass gradually fading, the life withering, as the cold Khumbu Glacier was approached. Not far from Thyangboche there was a collection of small buildings, perched on top of a hillock, with the track running beside them. A few sheep were grazing there, and an old bald and toothless crone, wearing the semblance of a monastic habit, exchanged a few unsmiling words with us as we passed. This was a Buddhist convent, said our Sherpas, inhabited, like the monastery, exclusively by persons of unfathomable purity and spiritual awareness. Half a mile farther on there was another settlement, this one swarming with gay Sherpa folk and their children, and brimming with gaiety. What was this, then? I asked the Sherpas. Oh, that was another place, inhabited by those monks and nuns whose purity had been plumbed after all.

Soon the track left the hill, crossed a stream by a stout Tibetan bridge, and petered into a wide and boggy green valley, overlooked by the savage peaks of Taweche and Ama Dablam. There were a few yak-herders' shelters, small square structures with enclosures for the animals; and here and there the valley was dotted with the statuesque figures of the yaks, who seemed to enjoy standing an alone in the wilderness gazing into eternity. I was invited to buy a yak, load it with all my equipment, drive it up the glacier to 18,000 feet, and then eat it; but they looked such gentle and longsuffering beasts, at once so tough and so cuddly, that I could not bring myself to do it. Instead, Sonam acquired some strips of yak-meat; and that night, as we sheltered in one of the huts, he cooked it and embedded it in a huge mound of mashed potatoes, garnished with a rare vegetable called a Thyangboche onion. It was excellent; and since I had brought with me several tins of malted milk, the day closed on a note of exiled domesticity, and one almost expected to see the Sherpas pinning their hair up or putting out the cat.

Next day we moved on to the glacier. It has been described a score of times since then, but in memory it is still a cold and disturbing place. A great mound of moraine rubble marked its course, and over this uncomfortable ground you had to jump and slither and slide your way, a tiring progression. Dotted over the landscape, and growing higher and thicker as you climbed, were pinnacles and castles of ice, standing erect from the ground; sometimes alone, like fingers of warning, sometimes in shoals or grottoes, so that you could wander among them as you would pick your way through the roots of a banyan tree. It was a grotesque and dispiriting place, made more disagreeable by the altitude. We were now at about 15,000 feet—an uncomfortable height for a newcomer. I found myself more and more breathless as we advanced, so that doing up a shoe-lace would puff me, and more and more reluctant to keep moving. The great mountains were so close to us now, on every side, that it was difficult to get pleasure from their beauty of form; and altogether the prospect was a bleak one.

On the glacier we met Hunt, who had come down from Base Camp, at the foot of the mountain. He was a weird sight, for his face was heavily coated with glacier cream, giving him the appearance of an eminent clown, or a performer in some barbaric glacier rite. (He was right to use the cream so lavishly. My own face, heavily bearded, like an anarchist's, was already splintered and peeling from the sun, and my lips were painfully swollen.) Hunt is an earnest and a serious man, a leader of genuine inspiration, a superb organizer, and a person of deep religious feeling. I hardly ever met him, throughout the expedition, without feeling flippant, as if I had somehow wandered into the Royal Society reading *True Confessions*. I had always respected H. W. Tilman's choice of a Chesterton quotation to preface his account of the 1938 Everest expedition: 'Still, I think the immense act has something about it human and excusable; and when I endeavour to analyse the reason of this feeling I find it to lie, not in the fact that the thing was big or bold or successful, but in the fact that the thing was perfectly useless to everybody, including the person who did it.' But one simply could not summon up this feeling in the presence of John Hunt. The thing might only be the climbing of a mountain, but under the touch of his alchemy it became immeasurably important; as if the fate of souls or empires depended upon getting so many pounds of tentage to a height of so many feet. He was authority and responsibility incarnate. Is there a Leader-Figure in the mythology of the psyche? If there is, he was its expression. As a doer of duty he seemed to me invincible; whatever job he was given, the building of a chicken coop or the translation of an Aramaic testament, he would first clothe the task in garments of unapproachable significance, and then proceed to complete it.

He told us that Hillary's party had penetrated the icefall, the great barrier of shifting ice-blocks that is the first and most dangerous obstacle of Everest. Hillary and the other New Zealander, George Lowe, were now at a camp farther up the glacier, and we would meet them next day. All seemed to be going well enough. The peak of Everest, now standing clearly above the Nuptse ridge, was grey and free from snow; but this was only because the severe spring winds were still blowing, driving the snow off it and guarding it impenetrably against intruders. There were, it seemed, only two short seasons in the year when Everest might be climbed—during the spells before and after the monsoon in which the mighty winds momentarily relaxed. What would happen, I asked Hunt, if the pre-monsoon assault failed? Would he try again in the autumn? He replied that Everest was reserved for the British during the whole of 1953, and there would certainly be an autumn attempt (after a period of reorganization) if the spring one failed; in England reserve climbers were already prepared for it. After that, it would be the turn of the French, who had permission to come to Everest in 1954. Hunt stayed with us for an hour or two, telling me what had happened already, and then returned up the glacier.

Our own slower progress, impeded by our columns of laden Sherpas and Sherpanis, was delayed by a change in the weather. The sun had been shining brightly till now, and the temperature was not unkindly; but late in the afternoon it began to snow. The glacier was veiled in misty light, so that the ice pinnacles peered at us suspiciously through the gloom, and the great mountains appeared only momentarily between the clouds. Big snowflakes drifted across our path, wet and cold, and soon the ground was thick with them, and the way all but obscured. Our camp site that night was beside a small lake, mysteriously unfrozen throughout the year, at about 17,000 feet, and by the time we arrived there we were a bedraggled company. The woollen cloaks of the Sherpas were soggy, and the coiled hair of their women clammy. Snow covered the packs upon their backs, and seeped through the bright embroidered wool of their Tibetan boots.

In such circumstances Lake Camp was a bleak and unwelcoming place. A couple of small tents were pitched above the lake, and from them there emerged to greet us the huge smiling figures of the New Zealanders, eccentrically dressed. Otherwise there was nothing except a few low walls of loose stone, behind which previous travellers had lit their fires. This was far above the line of habitation, and all was hard and lifeless. The snow had developed into a blizzard, driven fiercely across the glacier valley by a vicious wind. It was all very unpleasant.

The Sherpas, though, took it in their stride. Dumping their loads behind the rocks, they dispersed among crags and boulders; and in a few moments, from unlikely chasms and hidden holes there came the twinkling of camp fires and the smell of roasting potatoes. The women bustled as energetically as the men, their smiles as broad as ever, their voices just as raucous. When night came I stole out of my tent, huddling my windproof clothes about me, and walked silently about the camp, feeling like Henry V; there the Sherpas lay, bundled in their cloaks, curled up like husky dogs behind heaps of stones or boulders, sleeping peacefully as the snow piled up upon their bodies.

When we awoke next day the sun was brilliant again, and there was a new hazard to face. The glare of the sun upon fresh snow is dangerous, for the dazzle can temporarily blind a person, and be extremely painful. The sahibs of the party had their sunglasses and goggles, and so did the climbing Sherpas; but the poor rank-and-file, engaged simply to carry baggage to Base Camp, had no such protection. Already, before the march began, they were feeling the glare, and asking us for glasses. I distributed the spare goggles I had, and the climbers shared out their supplies; but there were nothing like enough for this army of 200 men and women. We improvised. Some of the Sherpas bound odd bits of coloured cellophane around their eyes. Some used pieces of cloth. Some shielded their eyes with newspaper. Some masked themselves with pieces of cardboard, leaving only pinholes for the eyes. Some simply bound their own pigtails around their faces, their eyes peeping through the strands. So, looking distinctly queer, we proceeded a little shakily up the glacier; and before very long a gentle film of cloud obscured some of the dazzle.

It seemed an eternity up that track, but at last we saw in the extreme distance a gathering of tents. A big pyramid tent in the centre was surrounded by smaller ones, and a little structure of stone had been roofed with canvas sheets to form a kitchen. The tents stood on a moraine hillock in the shadow of the Nuptse spur, so that you could see them from a long way down the valley. As we drew nearer we noticed a small figure in a

blue anorak in a gully to the right of it, and heard over the stillness of the ice an occasional snatch of conversation. But we
were not there yet. The top of the glacier is thickly littered with
ice formations, beautiful and sharp of edge, so that one was
always having to make detours, or scramble down into unsuspected depressions. I could see those confounded tents for half
an hour before at last I reached the final obstacle, a narrow,
slippery passage through an ice-block, and after a brisk and
self-possessed walk across the moraine collapsed into a tent. It
was merely the altitude that had exhausted me. The glacier was
not really difficult, and in later weeks, when I was better acclimatized, I used to romp up it like a clumsy chamois. But this
was the first time, practically direct from Victoria Air Terminal,
and I much enjoyed the mug of steaming tea they brought me.

I would not say that Base Camp, Everest, was a lovely spot.
It was too dead and aloof for beauty, rather as if some dread disease had passed this way, killing everything in sight, to be followed by some giant instrument of hygiene; so that the place
seemed first to have been effectively murdered, and then ster-
ilized. Directly above the camp was the icefall of Everest, a
tangled mass of ice, twisting round to the south to form our
Khumbu Glacier. The head of the valley was paved partly with
ice lakes and pinnacles, partly with piles of the dull moraine on
which the camps had been placed. All around, forming the
head of the valley, stood a magnificent cirque of snow peaks;
the best of them being Pumori, a serene and handsome mountain, given its name by Mallory.

High above our heads stood the most romantic of these marvels, the Lho La. This narrow col, between the bulk of Everest
and the peak of Lingtren, was the frontier. Beyond it was Tibet.
Its lip was lined with a thick overhanging layer of snow, looking as if a footfall might precipitate it into the valley; nobody
had ever dared to cross it. Bullock reached it from the other
side, in 1921, and photographed the then unknown southern

side of Everest. (In the same year Mallory peered at this place from another, neighbouring col; marvelled at the mountains of Nepal; and wrote happily in his diary: 'It is a big world!' Now nearly all the mysteries have gone, and there is scarcely an unknown country left to peer at.)

Camping at this place was rather like living among the mountains of the moon. The glacier stretched away to the south like a smear on a lunar map, and the stars seemed closer and clearer, and there was a sense of unreality about the adventure, now that the mountain was, so to speak, in camp with us. When the moon itself came up, jealous of its reputation, it glowed huge and brilliant among the peaks, glinting on all the battlements of ice that complicated the glacier floor. In the morning the sun was generally hot; in the afternoon the snow began to fail; at night the temperature was well below zero. Often there was a rumbling and tearing noise above us, and there on the mountainside would be a cloud of snow, ice, and crumbled rock, marking the progress of an avalanche.

We were many miles, and several thousand feet, above normally inhabited country; but there were a few indigenous creatures at Base Camp. The famous high-altitude spider, loftiest of insects, certainly lived among the rocks. Choughs flew over us, or pecked their way among the crumbs and potato peels of the camp. Once a flight of storks passed overhead into Tibet ('Going to fetch salt,' explained the Sherpas sagely). Scuttling among the boulders of the moraine one could even sometimes catch a glimpse of a tail-less Tibetan rat, an endearing brown creature rather like a hamster, with a sniffing nose and whiskers. Otherwise we were all human—the thirteen members of the expedition, the thirty or so high-altitude porters, a few peripatetic wives and children, and my own little band of followers. Odd people looked in from time to time, and there was a regular service of men bringing firewood to replenish the huge pile of sticks and branches that dominated (in its moments of repletion) the entire camp.

This would be my headquarters, to be identified by the news-paper dateline: 'Base Camp, Everest'. I pitched my tent a little apart from the others, for I did not want to seem importunate, and in it I rigged up my radio receiver, with its tall tripod aerial outside. It looked splendidly functional, and I found it handy for listening to Radio Ceylon, the most powerful transmitter in that part of Asia. My books, papers, and typewriter were piled about my bed, and underneath it, protruding rather uncomfortably through the canvas, were my containers of money.

Hunt had said that I must be self-sufficient, and I prepared to eat my own yak-meat in solitary grandeur; but somehow the scheme fell through, and tossing my tins into the expedition's pool, I took to feeding with them. At night we ate in the big tent, in semi-darkness, helped only by the flickering light of a lamp. In the morning we carried our eggs into the sharp sunshine, to sit on boxes and eat off packing-cases, watched by the tail-less rats. These were the early stages of the venture, and almost everyone was then assembled at Base Camp. The first reconnaissance team had penetrated the wilderness of the icefall and the route up it was now being marked, day by day, with small red flags. Next, when the way had been prepared with the necessary ropes, steps, and bridges, the sturdy Sherpas would begin taking stores to establish staging camps on the mountain.

Though I had wondered at the inventory in Katmandu, it was now brought home to me much more forcibly that climbing Everest was largely a matter of logistics. Scattered around us on the moraine was an extraordinary collection of things, all beautifully crated in boxes stamped with the words: 'British Mount Everest Expedition, 1953'. There was everything here from a sporting rifle to a pair of shoe-laces, the whole mass overshadowed by the innumerable oxygen cylinders which lay stacked in neat piles in a corner. Success on Everest depended upon getting the right amount of all this stuff at the right time to the right place on the mountain, together with fit and resolute men to use it. On one of my first evenings with the expedition I mastered this basic truth; for in the shadows of my tent I typed out, for distribution to the climbers, Hunt's loading tables—an intricate set of figures, dates, and weights much more reminiscent, I thought, of Camberley than of Chamonix.

For the moment these multitudinous supplies were lying in wait, and the climbers were probing and marking the icefall. Next morning I woke to the sound of clattering metal, and looking through the flap of my tent I saw two figures in blue windproofs passing by across the moraine. Michael Ward and George Band were leaving for the icefall. Round their waists were wound their climbing ropes. Goggles were pushed back on their foreheads. Their cheeks were white with glacier cream, above the stubble of their beards; their crampons, not needed until they were in the icefall, were fixed to the tops of their ice-axes, and they clanked as they walked like the armour of knights. Two small squires darted out to shake their hands as they passed by—Sherpas in down clothing, wishing them good luck; and so they clattered away, their voices echoing among the ice pinnacles, until they turned into the labyrinth and were out of sight.

Soon I would be following them, for I planned to make an early ascent of the icefall; but first I wanted to acquire some more general impression of the shape of the mountain. On the other side of the valley rose Pumori, heavily snow-capped. The lower part of its mass was of bare rock, with the scree of the moraine leading up to it, and it would be easy enough to reach a convenient ledge upon its flank and look across to the mass of Everest. Accordingly Sonam and I set out in the early morning to cross the glacier and climb it. It was a tiring job, for I was still unacclimatized, and the ridge I had chosen as our objective was at about 20,000 feet. The moraine was a bore, for it ran in high ridges intersected by slippery shaly gulches; it took a great deal of effort to cross it and begin the upward climb. By the time we were approaching the ridge, towards midday, I was so breathless that I staggered from boulder to boulder helplessly, bending over each big rock to pant my breath back; but at last we sat there, Sonam and I, and leant back to enjoy the view. We had brought some biscuits and jam with us; and from time to time, spreading a biscuit thickly with the confection, we would reach out a hand for a lump of snow, press it into a convenient block, and enjoy a sort of sickly ice-cream sandwich.

There it stood, this monstrous mountain; for the first time I could see it as a whole. It seemed to glower at me. Mallory said it was like a prodigious fang excrescent from the jaw of the earth; so sulky and brooding did it look that morning that I thought it must have the toothache. Great mountains surrounded it on every side, but it looked recognizably the greatest (and nastiest) of them all. The rock slabs of its upper slopes were almost free of snow, and only the thinnest plume was driving from its summit; it had a very cold and calculating look about it, as if it were working out the dentist's bill. We could see almost all the route first followed by the Swiss, and now to be retraced (with minor variations) by the British. First came the awful shattered wilderness of the icefall, a mass of broken, tumbled, tilting, shifting, tottering blocks of ice, intersected by innumerable crevasses, swept by avalanches from the rock walls on either side of it. It looked like a huge indigestible squashed meringue. Beyond it was the valley of the Western Cwm, a cleft cut in the side of the mountain, narrow and overhung, and sunk in an unearthly white silence. The steep mountain wall of Lhotse bounded it, rising as a precipice to the flat plateau of the South Col, at 26,000 feet or more. There the climbers would turn to the north, and make their perilous way up the long final ridge of the mountain. A small bump not far from the top was called the South Summit; after that a precipitous rock ridge led to the summit proper. We could see it all, from the minute tents of Base Camp, far below us, through the successive obstacles of the mountain, to the little empty dome of rock that was the target.

We could see more; for while the southern side was bathed in sunshine, expectantly, to the north we could see the Tibetan approaches to Everest, suggestively shadowy. This was the route of the old Everesters, from the glacier of Rongbuk to the North Col, and along wearing snow slopes towards the summit. There were all the landmarks of those old adventures—the first and second steps, the yellow band, North Peak—names familiar to whole generations of climbers and mountain-lovers. An invisible barrier of politics and prejudice shielded those places from us; all the same (it may have been the altitude, or the heat of the sun, or the cold of the snow) I fancied there were spirits watching us still, over the gateway of the Lho La.

We scrambled down the mountain-side again in the heat of the afternoon, scraping our shins on innumerable rocks, and sometimes slithering uncontrollably down the scree. It was an exhilarating descent. Near the level of the valley floor we suddenly found ourselves standing on the edge of a small tarn, for all the world like some isolated Welsh mountain lake, its water green and unruffled. There was no trace of ice upon its surface, and it stood there demurely, tucked away behind the moraine. Weeks later Tenzing noticed this little lake from high on Everest, and in 1954 members of an Indian expedition trying to climb Pumori set foot upon its banks. They claimed to be the first people ever to reach it, and gave it an Indian name. They were not. Sonam and I were the first, and its name is Lake Elizabeth.

Down we went, and when next I looked up from the tricky terrain there was the bulk of Everest looming above us. Its summit was hidden by the projecting North Peak, and I could see only the top of Lhotse above the vast frozen morass of the icefall. It looked as if you could lose an army in its secluded corners. For a moment, on my ridge of Pumori, it had occurred to me that if I stood up there on the day of assault, I might see the tiny figures of the victorious climbers high upon the very summit. Now I pondered again upon the gigantic scale of it all, and realized that if ever a pair of climbers reached the top of Everest, only the gods (and those watchful spirits of the Lho La) would be able to see them there.

5

Climbing

TOWARDS THE END OF APRIL I made my first journey onto Everest. The runners were performing smoothly, leaving at regular intervals with my dispatches, and generally doing the journey to Katmandu in eight or nine days. Between us, Hunt and I had described in detail the march out to the mountain, the period of acclimatization, the move up to Base Camp, the first reconnaissance of the icefall, the establishment of a route through its shifting dangers. It was time, I thought, to see something of life higher on the mountain.

I left one fine morning after breakfast, with Band and Westmacott, and followed them across the crisp, brittle ice-lane that led us, wandering through the moraine, to the foot of the icefall. There we roped up—three sahibs, four or five Sherpas. This was my introduction to mountaineering, and clumsy indeed were my movements as we moved off. If ever a rope could tangle, it was mine. If ever a pair of crampons would not fit, they were those kindly issued to me by the expedition. My snow-goggles were nearly always steamed up, making it extremely difficult to see anything at all. My boot-laces were often undone, and trailed behind me forlornly. Nevertheless, buckling my rucksack around me, and taking a determined grip upon my ice-axe, I followed the large, flat expanse of Band's back into the wilderness.

It would be foolish to say that I enjoyed this first climbing of the icefall, especially as I was still ill-acclimatized; but there was a grave fascination to our progress up so jumbled and empty a place. The icefall of Everest rises two thousand feet or more and is about two miles long. It is an indescribable mess of confused ice-blocks, some as big as houses, some fantastically fashioned, like minarets, obelisks, or the stone figures on Easter Island. For most of the time you can see nothing around you but ice; ice standing upright, as if it will be there for eternity; ice toppling drunkenly sideways, giving every sign of incipient collapse; ice already fallen, and lying shattered in sparkling heaps; ice with crevasses in it, deep pale-blue gulfs, like the insides of whales; ice to walk over, pressed and piled in shapeless masses, in alleys and corridors and cavities; like some vast attic of ice, at the top of a frozen house, full of the cold icy junk of generations. All this mass was slowly moving, so that it creaked and cracked, and changed its form every day; and from the high mountain walls on either side, squeezing the icefall together like the nozzle of a toothpaste tube, avalanches came tumbling down.

Much of the climbing of the icefall consisted of a precarious trudging through this frozen morass; for the newcomer a breathless process, relieved only by hastily snatched moments of rest upon the head of his ice-axe. Now and again, as we climbed, we could see through gaps in the ice-mass into the valley below, with Pumori growing small behind us, and Base Camp out of sight over the lip of the ice. Soon we were on a

level with the Lho La, and could see over it into the mysteries
of Tibet; they looked to me very like the mysteries of Nepal. On
either side of us, as the icefall narrowed, loomed the rock walls
of Everest and Nuptse, so that one felt hemmed in and vaguely
threatened. Sometimes we stopped for a rest and a draught of
lemonade from Band's bottle; but most of the time we trudged.

It was a dangerous place, the icefall, chiefly because of its
incessant movement. Our route was roughly marked by small
red flags stuck in the snow or in the flanks of the ice-blocks;
but here and there, deep in dangerous gullies, or high on inaccessible pinnacles, other flags were flying, tilting crookedly,
sad and tattered. These odd souvenirs had marked the Swiss
route in 1952, and it was poignant to see them now, so far from
a safe way, like little red Sirens in the ice—not least because
they had been provided by a munificent shoe manufacturer,
and still proclaimed the name of his product in what seemed
rather a forlorn kind of advertising campaign.

Sometimes our route lay up the steep side of an ice-block,
and there the Sherpas, with their heavy packs, would swing
wildly up a fixed rope, groping and scraping and clasping
hand-holds, until they were heaved up by their comrades at the
top and shook the snow off themselves as a dog shakes off
water. Sometimes we squeezed through minute cracks in the
ice, our packs catching and sticking, until we pushed our bodies through with an almost perceptible 'pop'. In one place we
had to manoeuvre ourselves through such a gap, slither down a
confined ice-slope, jump across a crevasse, and climb up the
other side. I floundered my way down this place, poised for a
few agonizing moments across the crevasse, wondering which
leg to move next, and somehow scrambled up the other side;
but during this process I felt my wrist scraping hard along an
ice-block, and when next I wanted to find out the time, I discovered that my watch had gone, down into the depths of the

crevasse. It was an automatic watch, wound up by the motion of my wrist; and I believe that it is still ticking away there in the blue vaults of the glacier, rocked and stimulated by the movements of the ice, inching its slow way down into the valley, still faithfully recording Greenwich mean time.

Often such crevasses were too wide to jump, and had to be bridged. The expedition had a few sections of aluminum ladder for this purpose, across which one picked one's way like a big spider. But there were many more crevasses than there were ladders, and most of them were bridged by another device: a greasy old pole, jammed into the snow on either side, like a huge toothpick jammed between molars. I found these poles unsympathetic. Each climber had to cross alone, his companions hanging on to the rope at either end; and the spikes of my crampons, which were generally loose anyway, used to stick into the wood in a disconcerting way. As often as not the pole would start rotating greasily in the snow as you picked your way across, and it was difficult to know whether to watch it rolling, or to let your eyes slide off into the great hungry depths of the crevasse below you, a hundred feet deep or more, cold and blue.

As the evening approached it began to snow, as it often did on Everest. In the sunshine the icefall could be a stifling place, for the heat was caught between the walls and pillars of ice, and was able (so few were the available targets) to pick you out personally for a roast. There was a particular malevolence about this heat, as if it were in league with all the other menaces of the place—the shifting blocks, the gaping holes, the greasy poles, the dazzle, the dulling altitude, the avalanches—and even the lovely blue sky and the sunshine seemed unfriendly. So I always welcomed the flat, soft wisps of snow in the late afternoon. They drifted idly at first, out of a blue sky; but gradually the day turned grey, the clouds thickened, and the great mountain masses were obscured. On went our windproofs, and through the rising snow we laboured, the moisture trickling down the backs of our necks; if we looked to the south, down the valley of the glacier, we could see battalions of wet clouds marching up towards us, far below.

Half-way up the icefall a small staging camp, Camp II, had been placed on a plateau jutting over the morass. This we reached comfortably just as the snow began to be unpleasant. I remember my first night at this camp with especial clarity. The mountain had seemed lifeless and impersonal till now, like a great slab of grumpiness; but the presence of this imperturbable little camp, perched there among the ice, suddenly gave the place a spark of life, and humanized the adventure.

There was a cheeky Cockney flavour, I thought, about the very existence of the place; and in the face of so gigantic and uncompromising an overseer as Everest, there was a new attraction in impertinence. I used to like to lie in my tent in such a camp as this watching a team of sahibs and Sherpas come toiling up the monster to the plateau. Over the ridge they would come, their tired bodies bent, with a little extra springiness entering their steps as they saw the tents ahead of them. Wearily they plunge their ice-axes into the snow, unfasten the rope with their stiff cold fingers, and untie (with many a hissed or muttered scurrility) the frozen straps of their crampons. The Sherpas hustle off to some of the tents; the Europeans, seeing that the supplies are stacked properly, into others. Then what a heaving, heavy blowing, bulging, rolling, and twisting ensues! Each tent is no more than three feet high, and it has a narrow sleeve entrance near the ground; into this small hole the tired climber must struggle, wearing awkward windproofs or thick down clothing. There is a maddening struggle with the flapping sleeve of the tent (the snow dripping, all the while, or blowing past in chilling gusts); boots get caught up with nylon tentage; rucksacks have to be dragged in behind, like stubborn fat terriers on leads.

Inside the tent is probably a little clammy, for it has been empty since the last party went this way. Litter lies about its floor—a bar of chocolate, a packet of breakfast food, a scrap of old newspaper. There is a smell of lemonade powder, wet leather, and chocolate. In one corner is a walkie-talkie set, a tangle of wires and batteries. Once inside this uninviting place, the climber twists himself about laboriously and slowly removes his boots, banging them together to clear them of clinging snow (I always remember the sound of banged boots, most redolent of Everest). He heaves his inflatable mattress from his rucksack, the tent bellying around him, and blows it up in a series of impatient gasps. He stretches it on the floor—it just fits in—and places his sleeping-bag on top of it. A few more contortions inside the tent, like a ferret down a rabbit hole, and into his bag, socks, down clothing, gloves, and all, the climber gratefully if ungracefully crawls. He uses his boots as a pillow; if he leaves them loose in the tent they will certainly be frozen hard in the morning, and trying to unfreeze a pair of climbing boots is a frustrating task. If he is far-sighted he has packed a book in his rucksack, for it may only be three or four o'clock, and the hours pass slowly. (The expedition carried a wide variety of literature. Wilfrid Noyce used to sit in the snow romping through *The Brothers Kara-mazov*. The two New Zealanders used to enjoy the ineffable respectability of the *Auckland Weekly News*. The official library ranged from *Teach Yourself Nepali* to Orwell's critical essays, with, oddly enough, not a single mountaineering book borrowed from the warped deal bookshelves of the Climbers' Club Hut at Helyg. I had a proof copy of W. H. Murray's *Story of Everest*, though, which we all read at one time or another on the mountain; everybody signed it for me, and it now stands in my library clad in a resplendent binding, its pages marked with the tea-stains and finger-prints of Everest.)

Before long the climber will be disturbed by a flurry and a commotion at the entrance to the tent, and a grinning Sherpa, puffing heavily in the cold, pushes in some food—pemmican, potatoes, a tin plate of mashed sausage meat. Sweet thick tea follows, tasting faintly of methylated spirits and strongly of the melted snow which provided the water—a taste, I used to think, desperately compounded of winds and desolation, for a rain-drop frozen on the slopes of Everest must be a lonely sort of thing. There may be biscuits and jam, packed in transparent packets like shampoo, or perhaps round slices of fruit cake, from a tin. It is not easy to eat delicately in a high-altitude tent. Sooner or later a mug will overturn, and a thin trickle of brown tea will settle into a puddle on the floor; crumbs innumerable crawl inside the sleeping-bag; where the blazes has that fork got to?

In the evening Hunt tries to link all the camps on the mountain-side with a radio call over the walkie-talkie sets. This demands some preparation. Batteries work better when they are warm, so they must be cherished inside the sleeping-bag, like teddy-bears, for half an hour before the appointed time; they are angular things, covered with odd protrusions, sockets, holes, and joints, and make uncomfortable bedmates. Then the tangle of wires in the corner must be sorted out, and the long flexible aerial, like a stage property sword, fitted into the receiver. At a pinch a determined man can do it all inside his tent, without once poking his nose outside, and Hunt's intricate instructions on the next day's duties can be absorbed in the warmth.

The call over, the cheerful good-nights sent winging up and down the mountain, and it is almost time for sleep. Everest keeps early hours; by seven o'clock the lights are dimmed and the camp is quiet, except for an occasional unaccountable spatter of conversation from the Sherpas. Now and then there is an enormous rumble, like a train crossing Hungerford Bridge, or the warning antique roar of the old elevated railway in

Manhattan, as an avalanche breaks and falls somewhere on the mountain ramparts. The climber disregards it; and swallowing a couple of yellow sleeping pills (for altitude often makes sleep difficult) he buries himself determinedly in his bag, muffled in thick clothing like a mummy among the ice.

Towards the end of dinners given in honour of the Everest party, months later and continents away, when the port was being passed, the ladies were absent, and the old gentlemen with their handsome white moustaches were beginning to warm up, somebody would generally remark that there was one question he had always wanted to ask about the expedition. He had always wondered, now—up there in the snows—it must be devilish cold—jolly difficult to move about, eh?—what happened in the night, now, supposing you—well, you know, supposing you were in that tent now, right up there, and—well, er, Nature called, so to speak? Tell me, now, what d'you do then? There was a copy-book answer to this query. The expedition was provided with small yellow plastic bottles, for this very purpose. But I was an outsider, and had no such bottle, and as the old gentlemen waited for their reply, I used to remember with a shudder those long hours of indecision and rising discomfort, the vagaries of procrastination and resolution, the self-reproach and reluctant preparation, the failing and resummoning of resolve, the twisting and turning out of the sleeping-bag, the fumbling with the tent-flap, and then at last the plunge outside into the sub-zero, in the middle of the night on Everest, with the moon harsh and icy, and the deep snow piling up against the tent! (How excellent was the brandy, how suffused the glow, of those long celebration evenings in London and New York!)

The second half of the icefall was rather worse than the first; and during that first wearying climb up its shaky platforms and avenues I had time to wonder why people wanted to climb mountains; though indeed my companions on that rope, the towering Band, the graceful Westmacott, looked as if they had no motives at all, but simply moved on to the mountain mechanically, like thoroughbreds led to a ring, and were doing (in the words of a forgotten song) what comes naturally. 'Because it's there' has a fine ring of finality about it, and spoken with a hint of sublime mysticism, as if there are bottomless pits of meaning yawning beneath the phrase, is calculated to hush the most importunate of lecture audiences; though I have often wondered if Leigh-Mallory, as human as the next man, did not spit it out in a moment of impatience, after being asked the same question thirty-three times in the same evening. Hillary's answer is almost as successful. 'I climb for the fun of it.' Nobody can complain of that. The simple sportsman can accept it at its face value; the moralist can rejoice at an honest man; the sycophant can tremble at the manly simplicity of it; the mystic-mountaineer can ponder the query 'What is Fun?' (between his indignant ruminations on the Ascent rather than the Conquest of his favourite mountain, it being a matter of faith with him, as I remember, that you must never be beastly to the thing).

Everyone, of course, does these things for a different reason, but I composed a formula as we climbed that might be applicable to most mountaineers. I believe their reason for climbing is partly pride (because they do not care to admit weakness); partly ambition (because a warm caress of glory surrounds the successful mountaineer, even if he only stands, alone and unhonoured, on some minor and ill-respected summit); partly aestheticism (because their sport takes them to such beautiful places); partly mysticism (because they wallow sensuously in a spiritual challenge); and partly masochism (because they actually enjoy the discomforts they undergo, crevasses, avalanches, cold, loneliness, squalor, fatigue, and all). Of these component motives it was the last that I found most convincing as we struggled up the mountain.

The snow fell again that afternoon as we slowly progressed through the maze, swirling and blowing about us and blurring the track we followed. We crossed a few more bridges and poles, slithered down a few more ice-slopes, swung up a few more ropes, squeezed through a few more crevices, and climbed up a rope ladder, respectably fitted with wooden rungs, like something at a Boy Scout camp. 'Presented by the Yorkshire Ramblers' Association,' Band shouted at me through the wind with an explanatory gesture, thus giving our venture an unexpected week-end touch. As the last glimmers of the sun disappeared and the gloom of evening arrived, we stumbled into Camp III: a couple of shapeless tents looking at us through the blizzard, a lonely wireless aerial, a pile of boxes half-hidden in the snow, an occasional sound of voices emerging murmurously from the darkness. I went into a thoroughly disused tent and, sweeping aside the miscellaneous junk inside it, lumbered into my sleeping-bag.

There was an especial satisfaction for me in resting that night at Camp III, Everest, at the top of the icefall. I was prepared to admit that journalists had written dispatches before from the altitude of Base Camp—18,000 feet; but I felt almost certain that no one had employed quite so lofty a dateline as this. But despite a certain elation, somewhere discernible at the back of my mind, I was never able to put much heart into my dispatches from such high places. It was not only that my head was generally aching, my limbs exhausted, and my fingers very cold; the altitude also has a dulling effect on the brain, blunting enthusiasms and antipathies, removing mental extremes, clothing experience in a grey and clogging uniformity. Judgement of distance and danger is warped, as everyone knows; but so are aesthetic values and standards of enjoyment and distaste. The great mountaineer, at the utmost limit of human endurance, unaccountably misjudges the safety of a corniche, like 'a sick man climbing in a dream'; the journalist, at his own level on the mountain, surrounded by the aura of great adventure, in the light of a golden Himalayan moon, can find nothing very memorable to write about.

As I dozed in my bag that evening, half-dreaming of tail-less rats and scrambled egg, in an agreeably muzzy coma, the flap of the tent was thrust aside and there appeared the enormous beaming face of Hillary, beneath an attractive striped linen helmet, rather like those worn by the Foreign Legion, kindly sewn for him by his fiancee.

'There's a nasty bit just down here on that last crevasse,' he said in a loud voice. 'I'm going down to cut a few more steps in it. What about coming and belaying me? D'you feel like it?'

His tone of voice was, I thought, distinctly *nonne*, or whichever interrogative it was they used in Latin to expect the answer 'yes'; and anyway I was too vain to explain that I was prostrate with exhaustion. So, heaving a long inaudible sigh, struggling out of my sleeping-bag, twisting and rolling to get my boots out, catching my feet in the flap, searching for my snow-goggles, I crept miserably out into the snow and followed him. I am glad, now, that he dragged me out that night; for I remember the incident as characteristic of Hillary, and illustrative of his supreme quality as a mountaineer. It was a horrid night, the snow driving and stinging, no moon, only the faint glow of reflected snow and the great shadow of Everest looming above us. I stood at the lip of the crevasse, the rope belayed around my ice-axe, while Hillary scrambled expertly down its face. There he worked in the half-light, huge and cheerful, his movement not so much graceful as unshakably assured, his energy almost demonic. He had a tremendous bursting, elemental, infectious, glorious vitality about him, like some bright, burly diesel express pounding across America; but beneath the good fellowship and the energy there was a subtle underlying seriousness; he reminded me often of a musician in the hours before a concert, when the nagging signs of nervous tension are beginning to enter his conversation, and you feel that his pleasantries are only a kindly facade. Hillary was as much a virtuoso as any Menuhin, and as deeply and constantly embroiled in his art; I first detected this strain of greatness in him that evening below Camp III, as the ice-chips flew through the darkness, his striped hat bobbed in the chasm, and I stood shivering and grumbling, all messed up with ropes, crampons, and ice-axes, at the top.

We awoke next morning to find the snow still swirling about us; but before we started the return journey we climbed a little higher to the entrance of the Western Cwm. I had seen this trench in the mountain-side from my eminence on Pumori, and wanted a taste of its atmosphere before writing my dispatch. We laboured up through the snow, crossing two deep crevasses, until we stood at the entrance to the valley; but alas, the air was thick with driven snow, forming a shifting, blinding veil. I could just make out the high rock ramparts on either side, and far in the distance I thought I could see the enormous form of Lhotse, at the head of the valley. But then if I had tried hard enough I could have seen anything that morning, for the snow-shielded Cwm was so redolent with mystery, its recesses felt so romantic, my head was so strangely befuddled by the height, and it seemed to me so infinitely improbable that I should be standing there on Everest in the snow. We sat down and drank some lemonade, and presently began our journey down the mountain.

I was almost the Everest expedition in microcosm; for my modest adventures paralleled the greater enterprises of the climbers, and I timed my own journeys up the mountain to coincide with the different stages of the attempt. Thus, when I was making my first climb to the head of the icefall, Hunt's reconnaissance parties were pushing ahead to the head of the Cwm and on to the vast slab of the Lhotse Face that rose above it. Similarly, soon after I returned to Base Camp to get my dispatches away and see to the organization of my runners, Hunt withdrew all the climbers from the mountain for a briefing on the plan of assault. This was a council of war before the attack on the summit. The groundwork had been done; quantities of stores had been taken up into the Cwm; the first examination had been made of the Lhotse Face; the time had come for a decision on the plan of final assault, and on the composition of the assault parties. Men would be made famous by this conference, and legends given birth. It was May 7, a significant date in the story of Everest.

Before the conference Hunt talked things over with Hillary and Evans, who had been made deputy leader of the expedition. He invited me to listen to this, and accordingly I tucked myself away in a corner as they hammered out the plan. It was a lovely sunny morning, and we basked there on the scree as we talked. When I heard that Evans and Tom Bourdillon, Hillary and Tenzing were to be the four men most likely to stand upon the summit, my first reaction was to wonder how their lives might be altered by the chance; whether, one day, Hillary's name would be as well known as Mallory's; and whether, indeed (a supremely selfish thought), they would all come back safely to tell me the news, or whether I should start thinking about obituary notices.

(Goodness, that was a thought! Had we anything in the morgue on the members of the expedition? What about portrait pictures? I must get a photograph of every member, so that if anyone disappeared irrevocably down a crevasse we could provide a reasonable obituary. Let me see, now, what code words did we have for catastrophes? 'Killed', 'Injured', and 'Ill' I knew we had arranged; it might be worth thinking up a few more, for the choice of perils was wide, and if someone was, for example, sucked permanently away by some unexpected subsidence of the ice, it might well be worth reporting.)

'There we are then,' said Hunt, smiling encouragingly at me, for he thought I had been working out rates of oxygen flow, 'we'll gather all the chaps in the dome tent in half an hour and tell them the plan. How about you, James, do you know all about it now?' 'Everything, thank you, John,' I replied, wondering if half a column would be enough for him.

But nobody was killed or maimed on Everest, and for this record Hunt himself was responsible. His planning was impeccable. He was no Gordon, for he was more tolerant than that fanatic commander; and fortunately no mysticism tempered the composition of his assault load tables. Nothing could be more cut and dried than the plan he now unfolded in the big dome tent. The sun had withdrawn by the time of the conference, and the snow was falling again. The wind alternately pushed and sucked at the canvas of the tent, and when from time to time some Sherpa entered, the doors shook and flapped like dervishes.

Almost everybody was gathered inside the tent, Tenzing stiff and upright on a packing-case near the door, the rest of us lounging on sleeping-bags, propped up against tent-poles, or sitting on the floor. Old newspapers were scattered all over the place, most of them tattered air-mail editions of *The Times.* As Hunt began his talk I watched the faces of my companions. Most of them were resolutely abstract or casual: Tenzing sat there inscrutably, graceful and attentive, like a demi-god on parade before Zeus. Three of us, at least, were relatively relaxed—Griffith Pugh, the physiologist; Tom Stobart, the movie-photographer; and myself—for we would certainly be in no assault party or crucial operation high on the mountain. For the rest, there was a distinct sense of excitement, and a sudden snapping of the tension when the two assault teams were named. First Evans and Bourdillon, then Hillary and Tenzing. I thought I saw the slightest flicker of satisfaction cross Tenzing's face, though in fact (we learnt later) he considered a Sherpa should have been in both parties; Hillary looked as if he had just been picked for the First XI, and was thinking about oiling his bat; Evans and Bourdillon reminded me of two unusually intelligent members of a board of directors, considering how to increase sales to Antigua. In a few moments, the plan was settled. Lowe, Westmacott, and Band would be responsible for cutting a way up the Lhotse Face. The movement to the South Col would be led by Noyce and by Charles Wylie, the gentlest and most English of them all. Hunt and Gregory would form a support party, to carry supplies up to 28,000 feet, if possible. Evans and Bourdillon would launch the first assault, using the new and little-tried closed-circuit oxygen; Hillary and Tenzing would follow if they failed, using the familiar open-circuit sets. Michael Ward, the doctor, was to act as reserve.

Had anyone any questions or observations? Hunt asked, looking benignly round the tent with a soldierly air, as if he were about to order his company commanders to synchronize their watches.

'Yes,' said Michael Ward, with a vehemence that nearly knocked me off my packing-case. 'I certainly have. I think it's a great mistake that you're going so high yourself. It's a great mistake. You've done too much already. You shouldn't go with that support team. I feel this very strongly.'

He spat this out with a flashing of eyes and a quivering of his saturnine head; and John thanked him gravely. The passionate doctor proved to be partly right. Hunt, who was forty-four, climbed extremely high with extraordinarily heavy loads, eschewing oxygen to save weight, and going to the absolute limit of his endurance; and of all the climbers he was the most exhausted, so that I used to wonder, after the event, looking at his tired, drawn face and thin body, moving with an air of infinite weariness, whether he would ever be quite the same again. But there, it was the sacrifice of leadership.

Ward himself was a distinguished climber as well as a physician, and in a way, of all those present in the tent, he was the

best qualified to offer an opinion on the plan; for if it had not
been for his vision we would not have been on Everest at all.
When, after the war, the Communists overran Tibet and the
northern side of Everest was irrevocably closed to Westerners,
the southern approach to the mountain (which we had followed)
was unknown. In 1921 Mallory, who saw the upper part of the
icefall from his col on the frontier, thought it doubtful that anyone could get up it. Thirty years later a pioneer Anglo-
American reconnaissance party, who looked at it from the
Khumbu Glacier, also thought it unlikely that there was a pass-
able way to the summit from the south. Thus for a time it
seemed that there was no possible post-war route to the top.
Ward, however, was the leader of a group of irrepressible mountaineers who believed that there *was* such a way, and who
pressed their views incessantly upon those dignitaries who
have power of life and death over Himalayan expeditions. Their
pressure led to a bigger reconnaissance expedition, in 1951; to
the Swiss expeditions of 1952; and to our present venture, now
reaching, as the wind blew and the tent shuddered, some kind
of uncomfortable climax.

The conference ended with mugs of tea all round. I withdrew
to my tent to write a long and technical dispatch; and there settled upon the whole party a new and closely knitted sense of
purpose. Not everyone agreed with Hunt's plan, for reasons too
complicated for me to explain; the forthright Gregory, for
instance, insisted that the first assault had no prospect of success and would fulfil no very useful purpose; but there was a
feeling that a new stage in the adventure had been reached,
that duties had been defined and opportunities distributed, and
that the direction of our efforts could now be seen more pre-
cisely. I sat on my boxes of treasure, typed out my dispatch on
my tumbledown typewriter, and wondered if anyone was interested at home.

Edmund Hillary, Everest 1953. © *Royal Geographical Society.*

The approach— Hillary on left. © *Royal Geographical Society.*

Hillary and Tenzing in the couloir (Lhotse face behind). *Alfred Gregory* © *Royal Geographical Society.*

Hillary on approach to Southeast ridge. © *Royal Geographical Society.*

Hillary and Tenzing about to leave the south couloir to establish Camp IX below the South summit, 27,200 feet. © *Royal Geographical Society.*

Tenzing and Hillary . . . after ascent. *Alfred Gregory* © *Royal Geographical Society.*

6

Sherpas

As the climbers slogged their way up the Lhotse Face, hampered by heavy snowfalls, I settled down at Base Camp for a week or more to ensure that my communications were working properly. Living night and day with my Sherpas, sharing their petty pleasures and annoyances, I began to acquire some insight into their strange exotic characters, and to perceive some vagaries of personality behind their brown faces, as smooth and as shining as nuts that have been polished on schoolboys' sleeves. They were a hearty, extrovert, boisterous people, and I always had to fight a feeling of slight repulsion at their overwhelming insensibility—insensibility truly in the grand manner overcoming all barriers of custom or manner, so that no secrets were inviolate and no idiosyncrasies protectable. If you have hidden habits, or eleven toes, or *Lady Chatterley's Lover* in your sponge-bag, do not go visiting among the Sherpas.

For generations the Sherpa porters, who had helped so many sahibs into the mountains, had been famous for their courage in adversity and for their unfailing good humour. Nobody had ever questioned their fundamental worth, brave, friendly, honest, strong, and loyal. All the same, a man is best judged at home, and until 1950 no European had ever penetrated to Sola Khumbu, where the Sherpas come from; the porters of the old expeditions were generally recruited in Darjeeling, where many Sherpas had set up home in the hope of finding more and better work. There were times, I confess, during my own stay in Sola Khumbu when I became no more than a reluctant admirer of the Sherpas, respectful indeed of all their high qualities, but weighed down with the burden of their heartiness.

For example, our first tottering march into the valley of the Dudh Khosi was made hideous for me by the jovial hilarity of the inhabitants. Oh, the plates of *chang* I drank, and the inexplicable jokes I laughed at, the dances I tried to dance, the backs I slapped, the girls I flirted with, the dear little children whose pranks I laughingly endured! Never a moment did I spend without a crowd of jovial Sherpas to watch me, thrusting their grinning heads between the flaps of my tent, poking their grimy fingers into the scrambled eggs, or simply standing staring, like that insatiable crowd on the veranda at Namche Bazar.

Once during the march I was walking happily up a river-side path, not far from Namche, when I caught sight of Sen Tenzing and Ang Nyima, sitting on the terrace of a house high above the road. They were both extremely drunk, and Ang Nyima was sitting in a kind of daze, an expression of indescribable foolishness blanketing his face. Sen Tenzing, on the other hand, was unnaturally animated. Waving his *chang* pan he jumped to his feet and shouted to me to join them. I was fond of the old rogue, so I foolishly accepted the invitation and toiled up the path to the house.

'Ah, sahib, this is the best *chang* in Sola Khumbu. In the whole of Nepal! There is no *chang* like this *chang!* The woman of this household is famous for it. Have some, sahib! Here, take this bowl, and you will find the *chang* inside the room there, over in the corner!'

I peered into the room, which was very dark, and could just make out some kind of container in the corner. There was a stifled giggle from the doorway.

'That's it, sahib! Over there, just open the lid and put the bowl in. Famous *chang* sahib! Take your fill!'

I opened the lid and put in my bowl, to find that the container was what used to be called, in more spacious days, a commode. Bacchanalian and uncontrolled was the laughter which now rolled in gusts through the open door. Sen Tenzing was splitting his sides; Ang Nyima was giggling a loose high-pitched giggle. 'Famous *chang* sahib!' said Tenzing, taking my pack off my back, getting out the tea, and preparing to boil a kettle. 'Now, would you like some scrambled egg, sahib, or some *chupattis* with marmalade? Here, sahib, let me loosen your boots!'

What can you do with such people, who throw a custard pie at you with one hand and make you a cup of cocoa with the other? Only count ten, and then say thank-you. For indeed their kindness was inexhaustible. Often and again I was pushed into the house of a perfect stranger for a meal, lavish in scale and (for a tired traveller, anyway) often delicious in quality. The Sherpa houses are well constructed on two stories, with paned windows and pleasant tiled roofs. They stand square, squat, and wholesome-looking, very different from the squalid shanties of the Katmandu valley. The ground floor is used as a storehouse, and in its gloom you are quite likely to stumble into a tethered yak, wheezing among the hay.

Up the rickety wooden staircase you go, the Sherpas leaping up it gaily, the sahib puffing and scrambling behind; and at the top you find yourself in what seems at first to be some kind of revival meeting or assembly of illegal saints. The whole of the upper part of the house consists of one long room, thick with beams and rafters, not unlike an Elizabethan cottage in England. It is dim and murky. A little light comes through the windows (unless they are piled too high with snow) and the rest comes from a large fire of yak-dung burning merrily in the middle of the room. Smoke from this fire swirls about, and from the outside you can sometimes see it seeping through cracks in the structure, like steam escaping from a Finnish bathhouse.

You may have looked forward, as you heaved yourself up the stairs, to a quiet evening beside the fire with your host, the two of you attended by his bustling but self-effacing little wife. Such is not your fate. The room is almost certainly packed to suffocation with Sherpas. Some are sitting on the floor, talking loudly to each other. Some are moving about carrying pots and pans. Some are poking the fire. Some are roasting potatoes. Some are feeding children. Some seem to be dead. Many of these people are members of the householder's family, many (like yourself) mere passers-by; but all are perfectly at home, and all equally facile in handling the baby. Don't be shy. Crack a joke or two as you join the assembly, or slip on a banana skin.

The walls of this big room are lined with trays, pots, pans, buckets, bowls, and other more obscure instruments of hospitality, and before long you will find yourself eating a splendid meal. The rowdiest old hag will prepare you a plate of boiled potatoes, spiced with salt from Tibet (and garnished with margarine from your rucksack). This is the staple diet of the Sherpas, and eaten beside a yak-dung fire, in the murk of a Sherpa living room, it can be delectable. There is *chang*, of course, in flat trays, very thick and sticky; or cocoa brewed by your own attendants; or perhaps Tibetan brick tea, most appalling of beverages. Soon you will feel content among these peasants, for all their loud high spirits, and lean back on your rucksack with a potato and a bowl of *chang*, the firelight flickering over your face, the chatter of Sherpas loud about you, the aromatic smoke curling around your head, like some replete barbarian monarch resting among his court.

The Sherpas, nevertheless, led a hard, exacting life. Their homeland was harsh and sparse, so unfriendly that they must move their yak-herds from pasture to pasture through the seasons. Sometimes they grazed them at 14,000 feet, at the beginning of a glacier; often they led them in convoy, carrying merchandise from India, over the 19,000-foot pass of the Nangpa La. Though many Sherpas lived in Darjeeling, in those days their own country had been little affected by western influences. There were no wheels in Sola Khumbu, except prayer wheels; no telephones, of course, or printing presses; no roads; no doctors; only one or two dark, secluded shops, selling the bleakest of little cheap trinkets. Theirs was a shuttered and anachronistic existence, tucked away in their beautiful inaccessible land.

I suppose it was this seclusion that led them to their worst excesses of boisterous bawdy when a foreigner appeared. No doubt to some deep-hidden cell of the Sherpa mind his arrival signalled a warning of alien danger, and set the Sherpa organism a-prancing with practical jokes. But indeed the very shape of the Sherpa seemed designed for horseplay. His dress was functional but wonderfully quaint, and his body was made for laughter. The Sherpa's face was round and brown (about as brown as a sunburnt Neapolitan's), creased and wrinkled with fun, with slanting Mongolian eyes and high cheek bones, the whole reminiscent of a slightly Oriental Toby jug. His stocky body was tough and agile, and extremely dirty. He wore a sort of shirt surmounted by a cloak. On his head was often a tall conical hat, gold brocade for the top of it, fur for the bottom, and on his feet were high embroidered boots, colourful with flowers and ornamental designs. What a sight he was as he came roaring down a mountain path, fit and supple as a goat, his face wreathed in welcoming smiles, drunk as a king from *chang*, the very embodiment of good fellowship and broad humour! Falstaff would have liked the Sherpas.

But oh! when the evening drew on, how the old Sherpa women screamed to each other through the dusk, like screech-owls in the woods! When they were young the Sherpanis were fragile and touching. Dressed in their gay aprons and Dutch bonnets, with flowered boots peeping through their long skirts, they stood on the outskirts of the throng, smiling faintly, their babies carried in boxes on their backs and totally smothered with blankets. They looked like fresh young sprites, from Alpine meadows. But middle-age fell upon the Sherpanis like thunder. Their faces soon became haggard and drawn, their voices inexpressibly awful. Swiftly their movements lost their grace, and their complexions their fresh mountain bloom. They would ogle you still, if you inadvertently allowed your eyes to appear above the rim of the chili bowl, and they were always ready with a chaff or a quip, which, hurled across the floor to an acquaintance on the other side of the room, whipped past you like a meteor. They never lost their brazen confidence, however advanced their state of decomposition; for the Sherpa men always treated them as equals, and they played an important or even predominant part in the affairs of the community. So who would not be a Sherpani? Beautiful in youth; desired in womanhood; a real scream in middle-age; respected and consulted until the final throes of dotage. Theirs was a triumph of enlightened feminism.

Almost every day, as I travelled through their country, the Sherpas annoyed me again with their irritating intrusiveness. Privacy was an abstract totally beyond their conception, and anyone might walk freely into anyone else's house. Nobody stole anything very much; everyone knew everyone else. It did not in the least surprise me, listening on the radio one day to

Dennis Brain playing a Mozart horn concerto, to find a whole covey of hill men bursting through the tent-flap to hear him too. Nor was I much put out, returning once to camp at Thyangboche, to find one of the oldest, dirtiest, and merriest of the lamas trying on my spectacles; he did not take them off when I approached, but looked at me for a moment, trying to get my blurred image into focus, and then sat down with a heavy bump on my sleeping-bag, convulsed with laughter. If he thought I looked funny, he should have seen himself.

But *au fond*, beneath it all, they were the most lovable and loyal of friends. For every moment of annoyance I had, the Sherpas gave me a hundred moments of pleasure. When the old harridan had done her screeching, she would lift her sixty-pound burden without a murmur and stride off through a blizzard onto a glacier. At any time of day or night your Sherpa would bestir himself to cook your meal, heat your water, carry your pack, climb your mountain. He asked no more than a reasonable fee, and perhaps any old pieces of equipment you had finished with; in return he would do far more than his duties required, giving you always splendid service and good company, and caring tenderly for your health. I spent some days with Sonam at his house in Chaunrikharka, recovering from a bout of illness; sleeping in a temple-room, in the company of eight hundred figures of the Buddha; visited throughout the day by swarms of curious well-wishers; fed with tough roast chicken and *rakhsi;* and treated always with great kindness and courtesy. Before long, I am afraid, the Sherpa as we knew him in 1953 will be a figure of the past, obliterated by fame, fortune, and foreign innovations; and I am glad to have caught a glimpse of him first.

Two moments in particular I cherish as characteristic of the Sherpa people at their best, away from the harsh hilarities of the valley. The first occurred at Base Camp one night, when I was sitting with Sonam and two other Sherpas by the entrance to my tent. It was a lovely clear evening, with the mass of the icefall looming like a phosphorescent cliff above us. We had been talking of the old days of Everest, the days of the old heroes—Mallory, Norton, Tilman, Shipton—and I had brought out from my bag W. H. Murray's book on the history of the mountain. Flicking through its pages, I came across a picture of the old Abbot of Rongbuk Monastery, on the Tibetan approaches to Everest, in his lifetime one of the most revered figures of Sherpa Buddhism, and a man of great piety and kindliness.

'Look there!' I said to Sonam. 'There's a picture of the Abbot of Rongbuk. Do you remember him?'

Sonam did not answer me, but took the book and looked fixedly at the page, gradually turning it, in a rotatory motion, from the upside-down to the correct position. At last he had it straight, and an expression of great seriousness and respect crossed his face. Putting down the mug he held in his other hand, he looked long and hard at the photograph, and then, very slowly, bent his head and touched the image of the abbot with his forehead. Slowly and in silence he passed the book to his companions, as an acolyte might pass the chalice, and in silence they made obeisance to it. The last man looked at it gravely for a few seconds after his gesture of salutation, shifting it slightly in front of his eyes as if that enabled him to see it clearer. Then suddenly he snapped the book shut and handed it back to me. The spell was broken; somebody stirred the fire; 'More cocoa, sahib?' Sonam inquired.

The second moment occurred one morning when I was travelling alone between Namche Bazar and Thyangboche, after a brief sortie from the glacier. The track wound its way around the hill-sides like a path on a Somerset moor, in pleasant heathland country. I was walking fast, for I was in a hurry to get back to Base Camp, and presently I saw far ahead of me another solitary figure, moving in the same direction. It was a robust Sherpa woman, wearing long aprons and a high embroidered hat. Despite her hampering skirts she, too, was making good time, striding healthily along the path, unimpeded by shopping bags or umbrellas; but gradually I overhauled her until, in a narrow bend of the track, I was able to overtake her.

She had given no sign that she knew of my presence, never turning round or looking over her shoulder, just ploughing steadily on like a colourful battleship. As I passed her, however, her left hand suddenly shot into mine; for a moment we touched; we neither of us spoke, and I was too surprised to stop; but I felt some small hard object pass from her hand into mine.

I looked down to see what it was, passed so strangely from traveller to traveller, and found it was a small brown nut. When I turned around to thank her for it, she grinned and nodded and waved me on; so I pushed ahead up the hill, cracking its shell between my teeth.

7

Practice

By THE MIDDLE OF MAY my sturdy runners were doing the journey back to Katmandu in astonishingly good time, urged on by a rate of pay that must have seemed to them quite Rockefellian, and which, I am ashamed to say, is alleged to have forced up prices in general throughout the Sherpa country. Their basic fee for the run to Katmandu (180 miles of difficult country, in the heat of summer) was about £10. This rate, I found, did not stimulate them to any notable degree of speed; it was what they earned for doing the journey at all. Accordingly I instituted a sliding scale, and this is what upset the Sherpa economic balance, almost forcing the Tibetan *sang* off the gold standard. If the runner took eight days or more for the journey he was paid his £10, no more; if he did it in seven days, he earned £15; and if he only took six days, he earned the fabulous sum of £20. I did not myself consider this amount excessive, for it was a tremendous feat of endurance and strength to run the distance

so swiftly, and nearly always my dispatches were delivered to
'The Lines' safely and promptly. Moreover, most of the runners
insisted on taking a companion, for company and safety, so part
of the money presumably had to go to him. Still, over the weeks
the expenses certainly mounted up, and there were some raised
eyebrows in London when I added to my account the charge for
a yak I had slaughtered for its meat. More brazen demands
have been made to newspapers, though; during the Abyssinian
War the *Christian Science Monitor* was presented by its correspondent in Ethiopia with a bill for two slaves.

The runners were certainly pleased with their earnings; but
I am sure they also ran so swiftly from a sense of loyalty. Two of
them, travelling alone, actually did the journey in five days, an
astounding achievement: an average of nearly 35 miles a day,
including the crossing of three mountain ranges more than
9,000 feet high, and a gradual diminution in altitude from
18,000 to 4,000 feet.

Sometimes, returning from their journeys, these rugged mes-
sengers would bring me small presents, generally stunted hen's
eggs wrapped in leaves. One man, scornful of the local *rakhsi*,
brought me supplies from Meksin, where the brew was especially potent, drinking a good deal of it on the way home, but
generally able to produce a cupful or two in the bottom of his
bottle when he arrived back at camp. They were a strange,
attractive company. Their faces were gnarled and smiling, and
they moved through the ice pinnacles like characters from a
fairy tale. I used to like to watch them setting off from Base at
the start of a journey. Off they would go from my tent, two odd
figures in high hats, voluminous cloaks, pig-tails, and woollen
boots, jumping agilely over the boulders and across the scree.
Men of an inferior breed would have stopped around the corner
for a smoke; but I knew that these people would keep moving
steadily through the hills until their task was done, sleeping in
caves, houses, or the shade of trees during the midday heat,

travelling silently through the night. There they would go down
the glacier; and on the last ridge beyond the camp they would
pause for a moment, turn, wave me a farewell, pat their chests
to show that the dispatches were safely immured inside their
cloaks, and then lope out of sight down the moraine: two
unlikely mountain men, travelling to Katmandu with the news
from Everest.

They were often stopped and questioned on the way, and I
was later given a pleasant description of a well-known British
correspondent who had lured one of these wild figures into the
bar of the Nepal Hotel, and was vainly trying (with the help of
a whisky or two) to extract some information from him: like
interrogating an unwilling ant-eater. For by now our competitors were active indeed, and by almost every returning runner I
had a sombre bulletin from Hutchinson, warning me of the
intricate nets laid across the way to catch our news. The monitoring stations were monitoring hard. The Sherpas were being
intercepted and pumped. Every scrap of rumour from the
mountain was being seized and elaborated upon. My own dispatches were picked up after publication, sent back to
Katmandu, and rewritten for use elsewhere. The outgoing
cables were filched. Once a mail-bag arrived at Katmandu with
its lock broken and its bearer, one of the expedition's runners,
reticent.

But so far as I could tell, nobody was getting the news before
The Times, thanks partly to our simple ciphers, which we never
used twice; and my dispatches were now appearing in the paper
seven or eight days after they left Base Camp. The mechanics
of the operation seemed to be efficient; but it was, of course, not
the progress of the expedition that chiefly interested our competitors, but the outcome. What worried me more than anything
was that Izzard or somebody else might arrive at Namche and
firmly appropriate the wireless station there; or worse still, that
a correspondent might actually come to Base Camp bringing a

portable transmitter, with which, when news of success or failure came down the mountain, he would flash a message to Katmandu in the twinkling of an eye. My Sherpas, sensing that I had this interest in the arrival of strangers in that country, constantly brought me rumours of unknown travellers approaching Sola Khumbu. Two distinguished English clergymen, they told me, had mysteriously arrived at Meksin and had set up camp on the high ridge overlooking the village; try as I could, I could summon up no convincing mental vision of such unexpected visitors, squatting there in their vicarage hats, spreading Gentlemen's Relish on their *chupattis;* but anyway they faded, and the runners' descriptions of them grew more and more confused, and their images grew less and less probable, until one day a Sherpa told me that it was all a mistake, and there had never been two distinguished English clergymen at all. Then there was an American lady, alleged to be looking for rare flowers in the country below Namche; and a sinister party of strangers rumoured to be approaching the Nangpa La from Tibet; and a perpetual blurred representation of Ralph Izzard, who was always being reported somewhere or other, coming or going, climbing or descending, like some misty figure of allegory; and finally one evening, like a shot from a cannon, the firm announcement that a big party of Indians, including a newspaper gentleman, had that very morning begun its march up the Khumbu Glacier!

This was undeniably alarming. The expedition had reached a crucial and exciting phase. A route had almost been established up the brutal face of Lhotse; soon, if all went well, a camp would be established on the South Col, and in ten days or so the first assault would be launched. The thought of this party of marauders advancing inexorably up the glacier made me nervous. What were they like, I asked? What kind of equipment were they carrying? Well, said the Sherpas, there was Mr.

Tiwari from the Indian radio station at Namche; and that big Sikh with the black beard, you know the one; and some Indian policemen; and the gentleman from the press, an Indian too, who had cameras slung all over him, like a saddled yak, ha! ha!; and they had tents and sleeping-bags and boxes, as if they were planning a long stay; oh yes, and one of the policemen had a big box thing on his back, very heavy, rather like *your* box, sahib, that you listen to the music on, only different; and Mr. Tiwari looked rather tired, they thought, but the press gentleman was going well.

Through the long hours of those glacial days I waited for the arrival of this cavalcade, and peered anxiously down the moraine for a first glimpse of that ominous box, which could only be, I thought, a radio transmitter—perhaps, indeed, the Indian transmitter itself, upheaved for the occasion, bicycle and all. How ignominious a conclusion I foresaw for my adventure, with *The Times* hopelessly beaten on its own story! As the days passed, and there was no sign of them all, I instructed each of my runners to put it about, farther down the valley, that if any radio transmitter appeared at Base Camp it would inevitably be destroyed with an ice-axe by that ruthless correspondent sahib up there; and I threatened them all with instant decapitation if they told anyone of events on the mountain. Nevertheless, the ferocious image of myself thus propagated did not prevent the arrival of the Indians; for one cold afternoon I saw a few humped, weary, dejected figures approaching the camp, with many a breathless halt and heaved sigh (how well I remembered mine!) and many an anxious searching for signs of hospitality. The competition had arrived.

Of this unwelcome party, much the freshest and most cheerful was the correspondent, a likable Bengali who had been engaged by a London paper to undertake this adventure. Mr. Tiwari lowered himself on to a packing-case with heavy gloom; he was feeling the altitude badly, and I stuffed him hastily with aspirins and tea. The big Sikh, in his fur-lined jacket, was tired but seemed to be enjoying himself; though he was stationed at Namche he had never penetrated to such harsh mountain places before. Two other Indians, they said, had fallen behind on the glacier would be arriving later. (Oho! said I to myself. The men with the transmitter!)

They had a number of Sherpa porters with them, and I was afraid that if these men came into close contact with the few expedition Sherpas then at Base Camp, they might well obtain some information from them. So with an unpardonable assumption of authority, as if I were Lord of the Glacier by some antique but ill-defined writ, I ordered them to set up their camp as far away as possible from mine; and our Sherpas were commanded, on pain of ghastly disfigurement, not to talk to theirs. I do not normally behave in this autocratic way, except at the breakfast table; but I was given a certain spurious position of superiority by our respective degrees of fitness. The Indians, poor things, were naturally exhausted from the altitude, even the policemen, who lived all the year round at 9,000 feet; but by now I was at the very peak of my physical form, all surplus weight discarded, my muscles trim, my wind excellent, my brain (at 18,000 feet, anyway) relatively clear. So I issued my brazen directives without much fear of contradiction; and sure enough, they were obeyed. Mr. Tiwari soon withdrew into his tent anyway, only anxious to get some sleep; so did the big Sikh; and the correspondent and I settled down for a most agreeable evening over the *rakhsi.*

However, as the night came on it occurred to us to wonder what had become of the other Indians, who ought surely to have found their way up the glacier by now. It would soon be dark, and the moraine would then be dangerous, and the men, who had no tents or sleeping-bags, would soon begin to feel the cold. I thought we ought to look for them; so summoning a few of our Sherpas I set off down the glacier. The moon was up, and lit the ice pinnacles with a ghostly shine. The air was deathly still and silent, and our feet crackled on thin ice or stumped and slithered over the boulders. One of my Sherpas had brought a primitive horn with him, and from time to time as we walked he would blow a thin blast upon it, which echoed, silvery and haunting, up and down the glacier, rebounding between the mountains. We shouted, too, and our voices swept away down to the south, into the valleys; and we shone our torches into the gullies, so that from a distance the glacier must have seemed alive with spirits. At last we found them, two or three miles from camp, already huddled together on the scree under their overcoats, like big woolly animals hibernating in a hole.

As they rose creaking to greet us I looked hastily at their baggage, piled beside them in the gloom. Thus I reaped the reward of virtue. No radio was there, and the only box I could see was a large metal tin, obviously intended to contain onions and ham sandwiches on some forgotten foray of Skinner's Horse. We wandered slowly back to camp, and found our two companies of Sherpas dutifully maintaining their segregation.

The Indians left next morning. If they had planned to make a long stay at Base Camp, they had changed their minds. Mr. Tiwari did not look at all well, and was probably anxious to get back to his duties. The correspondent seemed unaccountably reluctant to stay any longer, but asked if I would show him a place from which he could photograph the icefall. I took him to the top of a neighbouring hillock, and from there we looked together up the immense white cascade of the ice. He produced a telephoto lens and took some photographs. I let my eye wander farther, to the tip of Lhotse, just protruding above the icefall, and wondered how the climbers were faring up there, whether the Lhotse Face had defeated them, or whether there was now a camp on the South Col itself, 26,000 feet above sea-level.

That night I had news from the Western Cwm. Each evening I climbed to my vantage-point on the moraine to talk by radio with Hunt. I did not always succeed. Sometimes the atmospherics were too bad. Not all the camps were in communication with each other, because of intervening ridges or buttresses. Sometimes, if batteries were not properly warmed, the transmitters were not powerful enough. Sometimes one could hear a faint thin voice out of the void in snatches and jerks, alternating with long silences or horrible twitching noises. Sometimes you could hear them, but they could not hear you, the most maddening situation of all. That evening, though, contact was established, and I heard that the Lhotse Face operation was not going well. The slope was proving dreadfully difficult, and the climbers were having trouble in preparing any kind of route. Each morning they would cut their laborious steps and fix their ropes; each afternoon the snow would fall mercilessly and obliterate their efforts. For the moment the whole expedition was marking time; until the South Col was reached and stocked with supplies, there could be no thought of an assault on the summit. There was a possibility of complete failure.

'Come on up,' said the voice, 'there's plenty of room at Camp IV and you can see for yourself. And if you're coming, James, you might bring me a spare length of wireless aerial, and a few bars of chocolate, and *The Times* if you've got any new ones, and any mail of course—oh, and in the wireless box you'll find one of those large interlock spanners, thanks very much. Goodnight!'

So I did. Michael Ward, after a short visit to base, was going up again; and Stobart was going to take some shots of the icefall; so we travelled together, Ward in the lead, Stobart holding up the climb from time to time to leap on to some adjoining pinnacle and film us in action. He had just recovered from a bout of pneumonia, with a brief convalescence farther down the glacier, but he was a wiry, resilient person and an able climber, and pursued his purposes indefatigably. The fiery Ward endured the consequent delays fairly patiently, and trying to ignore the queer goings-on behind him (the cameraman choosing a likely small crevasse to jam his tripod into, the correspondent inextricably tangled up with his crampons and the rope) climbed doggedly upwards.

It was an unpleasant day. We did not stop at Camp II, but plodded on through thick snow to the head of the icefall. There was little to be seen of any route, for the snow lay thickly over everything, and Ward had to prod and feel his way through the dangerous parts with great caution. He was a slender, lithesome man, and it always gave me pleasure, even in those disagreeable circumstances, to watch him in action; his balance was so sure, and his movements so subtle, that when he turned his grinning and swarthy face upon you it was as if someone had drawn in a moustache upon a masterpiece by Praxiteles. Our progress was slow, and was later immortalized in a sequence in the film *The Conquest of Everest*, which magnificently illustrated the discomforts of the afternoon. We crawled into Camp III at dusk.

The weather changed for the better; and when we awoke next morning and climbed to the extreme rim of the icefall I found myself looking into a Western Cwm dazzling with sunlight, blue skies, and crisp, clear snow. How different from the first time I stood at this spot, and peered through that blizzard into an angry rock-rimmed maelstrom! Now all was sharp and sparkling. The sky was flawless, but for two streams of snow and vapour blowing away from the tips of Lhotse and Everest. The surrounding mountains were beautifully defined, and the shadows of ridges and boulders were black and abrupt. At first I thought there was something fundamentally cosy about the Western Cwm, tucked away in the side of the mountain there, protected by the vast ramparts of Lhotse and Nuptse, sheltered from the gales that swept over the South Col, guarded at its western end by the gracious sentry of Pumori. If it were not for one or two insuperable disadvantages, I thought, it might have been a nice place for a picnic; there was something distinctly homely about it.

This feeling wore off. Later there grew upon me the sensation that there was something distorted and unnatural about the Cwm. It was certainly secluded and protected; but it was so terrifyingly big. The wall of Nuptse rose above it like some vast impenetrable barricade, huge beyond description, three miles long and 25,000 feet high. An unimaginable thing! The rest of the Cwm, too, seemed after a time to be swollen and distended, like something in a feverish dream, and it had a certain devilish precision of awfulness, as if Nature had for once forgotten to smudge the line. But there, I was never properly acclimatized during my visits to the Valley of Silence (as the Swiss theatrically named it), and this is the Cwm seen through sick eyes.

It was a long wearying walk up the floor of the valley. The gradient was not steep but the altitude was considerable and in the middle of the day the sun was scorching. Tedious crevasses, zigzagging across the Cwm, intruded irritatingly into the way, so that you had to follow their meandering courses sideways across the valley until you found a place to cross them. Here and there, spattered on the snow, lay rocks and boulders that had come tumbling down from the heights above. It was a dead and empty place.

Camp IV was placed towards the head of the Cwm, in the shadow of the northern rampart of Everest. After marching up that high desert of snow I thought its little tents looked ominously like a mirage; but it existed all right, and in a sort of tent-shanty, its sides open to the air, I found John Hunt, ghastly with glacier cream, wearing a linen hat with its front brim turned up, and busying himself with some intricate technical problem of weights and measures. I sat down beside him, and ate fifteen of the Swiss Ryvita biscuits which had been found buried in the snow up there from the previous year's expeditions. Washed down with lemonade, they were perfectly delicious.

Our fortunes had improved a little since our conversation on the radio. For the first time the afternoon snowfalls were not coming as high as the Western Cwm, and work on the Lhotse Face had been rather easier. Behind us that day we could see great banks of cloud rolling up the Khumbu Glacier, about to unload themselves like possessive matrons upon Base Camp and the icefall. But they would not rise as far as the Cwm. For the first time for many days, the weather was smiling shyly at us. Hunt handed me his binoculars and told me to inspect the face of Lhotse, high above us. Far, far away up its crenellated mass, all crinkly with crevasses, *seracs*, snow-ridges, and miscellaneous bumps, I could make out two minute figures crawling ant-like against the white. Lowe and the Sherpa Ang Nyima, who had sown his wild oats so blatantly on the march out, were at work on the route. They laboured up there for ten days, an unprecedented time at such an altitude, and later climbed higher still in support of the assaults. Now their pace was slowing, and their effort was running down. The way was established more than half-way up the face, but no route had yet been cut to the South Col. It looked a long, hard, cruel way up there; the figures on the face seemed pitiably small and slow; and the sky looked limitless.

'Keep your fingers crossed for the weather, James,' someone said; and so I did, through the succeeding days, crossing my fingers, touching wood, throwing salt over my shoulder, entreating all the divinities supposed to hover about the summit of Everest to keep the snow and the wind away.

I was always anxious, during these sorties up the mountain, that something terrible might be happening at Base Camp. More competitors might have arrived. My runners might have struck, leaving me without any communications at all. Somebody might have stolen the treasure chests. So having seen something of events on the Lhotse Face, the great obstacle of the moment, I returned to the glacier and resumed my routine. You might suppose that in that bleak camp, far from normal human habitation, living generally alone with Sherpas, the time would begin to drag; in fact, the days slid swiftly by. In the early morning, when the sun broke brightly on my tent, suddenly heating the interior as effectively as if a radiator had been turned on directly beneath my sleeping-bag—in those bright early mornings I would listen to the news on the wireless, sometimes from London, generally from India, or lie for a few minutes pleasantly stupefied by the banalities of Radio Ceylon (one of its regular radio programmes began with a song called *Beyond the Blue Horizon*). Then breakfast, scrambled eggs in the sunshine, with the Sherpas chatting and eating noisily about me; a wash and a cleaning of teeth, in a flat round basin perched precariously on a packing-case, and often slopping over into my tent. If there was a dispatch to write that day, I would do it in the open air, with the typing paper flapping and tearing in the wind, and the carbon getting caught in the typewriter carriage, plied with frequent cups of tea or lemonade, and watched with cock-eyed astonishment by a few chirpy black choughs. (If only they could talk, I used to think, and tell me what they saw up there! Or run my errands for me up the icefall!)

There followed the briefing of runners; the payment of an advance of fee; the handshakes and expressions of gratitude; the public sealing of envelopes; and that little routine of farewell that I have already described. Soon after the runners left there often arrived a team of Sherpas from the mountain, generally led by a sahib; and with a clattering of crampons and a gay swinging of ice-axes they would stride into camp like heroes. Sometimes they would bring a note with them asking me to send up some wire, or radio spares, Grape-Nuts, crampons, or cocoa. Often they would bring a little scribbled page of information, dashed off by a kindly climber in a moment of leisure.

Sometimes in the afternoon I would set off alone for an exploration of the upper glacier. A lake of ice stood to the west of Base Camp, guarded by terraces and battlements of ice; but if you squeezed and scrambled through the pinnacles, and scrunched warily across the ice, you could soon find yourself among the great cirque of mountains that blocked the Khumbu valley. It was very symmetrical, this great horse-shoe of peaks, and with the glacier valley itself running down in a wide strip to the south, the whole formation reminded me strongly of those oblong strips of wood, with rounded ends, that used to slide into the tops of children's pencil boxes. Sometimes I struggled a little way up the side of Pumori, and looked again over the icefall into the Cwm, and gazed long and hard at the Lhotse Face through my binoculars. (A colleague in London had lent them to me, in return for the camera I lent him to take to Greenland the year before.) It all looked unutterably lonely and deserted; and as the days passed, and the weather shone upon us, I thought Everest itself looked ever more scornful and muscular, a wrestler doing a few exhibitionist contortions before weighing in.

Each evening at seven o'clock came my radio call from the mountain. Snuggling the batteries inside my windproof jacket, I dutifully climbed my hillock in the moraine and switched on. In the early days I laboured up each evening with the radio set; later I deposited it there in a wooden box, like a cache of gold. The voices on the wireless were still wispy and unpredictable and interspersed with crackling, bubbling, and squelching noises. Sometimes I could hear half a conversation—somebody at Camp IV, for instance, talking to Camp VI on the Lhotse Face—and it was rather eerie to hear the distorted silence that represented the other half of the dialogue. Often, though, a voice (generally Hillary's) would boom cheerily over the earphones like a busker at a fair. The expedition's radio procedure was terrible; but I soon swallowed my remnants of military pedantry on the matter, and sank easily into their slipshod.

Finally, gobbling down a plate of boiled potatoes, cooked in their skins and deliciously complemented with margarine and onions, I went to bed. The nights were cold and silent, the moon full, and the stars crystal clear; and I would generally only be disturbed by the rumble of an avalanche above me or the sudden disconcerting shuddering of the ground, accompanied by a clatter of displaced stones, that proved our little camp to be pitched upon a moving glacier.

After only a few days this placid routine was sharply interrupted. Everything suddenly happened at once. First there rose another of those misty disturbing rumours about the approach of a stranger. Again there loomed the spectre of a radio transmitter flashing out its messages there at Base Camp, before my eyes, with the high-altitude Sherpas crowding around it like excited children, and pouring into its receptive mechanism all the latest news from Everest. Frantically I repeated my warnings about the ice-axe; hour after hour I dinned into my poor Sherpas the need for secrecy; and before long, just before tea one overcast afternoon, I saw emerging from behind a distant ridge, like a seal rising for air, the head of Peter Jackson, special correspondent of Reuters and an old colleague of mine. For a moment I saw myself in a quandary. I was, perhaps, prepared to prevent any total stranger sending wireless messages from base; but Peter Jackson, well, he had never been anything but kind to me. . . . But all was well; when his body followed his head, to be followed in turn by a small and dead-beat company of Sherpas, I saw that he was travelling very light, and certainly carried no radio.

It was a happy encounter, Jackson was fit and gay, and we ate a large tea together. He had no intention, he said, of spending a night with me, but planned to return that evening to the glacier lake, and thence to Thyangboche. There he had rented a monastery house, from which he sprang like a spider each morning to intercept my runners; but they were honest men, and he the most scrupulous of correspondents, and they told him nothing. What about Izzard? I asked. Any news of him? Again he was reassuring. Izzard had indeed gone down to Calcutta, and had returned to Katmandu; but he showed no signs of coming to Everest again. And Mr. Tiwari at the radio station? 'He's always very pleasant,' said Jackson, 'but I don't see too much of him.' I never liked Jackson better than I did during this conversation; and when he did in fact leave the camp, just as he said he would, my heart warmed to the man; I even wished him luck, I remember, as he started boldly down the glacier. I was to see him once again before the end of my adventure.

Soon I was presented with another agreeable surprise. There was by now a feeling of rising tension and excitement in the air—even the choughs, I thought, hopped about with an extra portentousness. All of us, Sherpas and sahibs, shared this feeling of expectation; and I was not surprised when one Sherpa, detaching himself from a team returning from the Cwm, strode across to me and handed me a crumpled note, a brilliant smile splitting his grubby face. It was from Noyce. He had reached the South Col, breaking through the barrier of the Lhotse Face. Camp VIII was established at 26,400 feet. Now the assaults could go in.

Noyce's scrawled little note was like a message from another world, if only because it described his feelings at reaching one of the most desolate spots ever visited by man. As I read it in the sunshine I found it all too easy to envisage the scene up there, high above the Cwm, a little bleak wind-swept plateau swept free of snow by the constant raging wind, and open to the elements on either side. Noyce had climbed slowly up the last feet of the Lhotse Face and peered over the ridge onto the Col. There he saw a creepy sight. In the middle of it, among the stones, there was a tent—a ghost tent, or skeleton; a few bare bent poles, a few tattered shreds of material flapping in the wind. It was a memory of the Swiss climbers who had been there in 1952, the only other humans to reach this appalling place. The wind howled about him as he looked; and presently, securing the route as they went, he and his companion, the brave Sherpa Annulu, returned to camp on the Lhotse Face. 'It was a slightly uncanny sensation,' said Noyce's note; and somehow the dirty texture of the paper, the rough scribble of the writing, the wind that seemed to impregnate the message itself, made me shudder as I read. But the Sherpa messenger, perhaps noticing I looked a bit queer, shook me by the hand again and laughed aloud, before peeling off his snow-flecked sweater and stumping away to find some food.

This was fine news, and I sent it off to Katmandu post-haste. Hunt's plans had been delayed by the brutal conditions on the Lhotse Face, but there was still no sign of the monsoon, which would have put paid to the attempt, the snowfalls were still staying low, and the wind had abated a little. The sky was blue and serene that day, and the summit looked almost inviting. Few of us thought Evans and Bourdillon would reach the top, handicapped as they were by untried oxygen equipment and by the circumstances of their assault: indeed, Hunt had always called it a 'reconnaissance assault.' But they would be preparing hopefully for their effort now, and in a day or two Hillary and Tenzing would be following them from the Col, with Hunt, Gregory, and Lowe to set up the highest camp in the history of mountaineering—Camp IX, at 27,900 feet. It was all very exciting. I blessed Jackson for leaving us so quickly, and blessed Izzard for not coming back, and uttered an invocation in favour of Mr. Tiwari, whose unwitting help, I thought, would very soon be needed.

One more excitement hurled itself upon me at this lively time. When I climbed up my hillock, warming my batteries, and extracted the radio from its cache, it was Band whose voice reached me, in a surrealistic sort of way. We talked with difficulty of this and that; of the South Col and the first assault; of the weather broadcasts sent specially to us each evening by the BBC in London. I had missed the forecast of the day before, and I asked him what it said.

'Oh!' said he. 'If you didn't hear it, congratulations on *bubbly bubbly* your *switch switch!*'

'What?' said I. 'Can't hear you!'

'Congratulations your *wheeeee zugazug!* Jolly good show! They put it in after the forecast, you know!'

'I really am terribly sorry, George, but I simply can't hear you!'

'Your *sugsugsugsug!* Your *switchabubblebubble!* Your s-o-n!'

My *son!* So I had another son! I must make a note of that.

8

Snowmen

ONLY A FEW DAYS to wait, for success or failure! Long and intimate were the conversations I had with my Sherpas during these hours of suspense; and so charged was the atmosphere with mystery and excitement that often enough our talk would turn to that celebrated Himalayan character, the Abominable Snowman *(Homo niveus disgustans);* or, as the Sherpa people called him, the *yeti.* Since then expeditions have gone to the Himalaya specifically to solve the problem of this legendary creature, but the Snowman remains no more than a legend still, with little but his occasional great squashy footprints in the snow to mark his presence. On our expedition we saw nothing of him; somebody heard a strange whistle on the glacier which was said to be a *yeti* call; innumerable tales about him reached us from the Sherpas; but he only hovered about us shapelessly, never, alas, assuming any tangible form, merely flitting clumsily in and out of our conversations.

The Khumbu Glacier seemed to be ideal Snowman country, and sometimes I would wander off into its gullies and ravines hoping to catch a glimpse of some shaggy Snowman head, and wondering what on earth I would do if I chanced to stumble across a family of them: throw stones at them? run away? hide? I hugged my camera determinedly on these outings, but never a shaggy head did I see, nor hear the cavortings of any baby Snowmen. All the same, it was rather eerie creeping through those grim alleys among the moraine with not another human being for miles, only the little tail-less rats scurrying about the scree; in a silence only broken by the creaking and grinding of the glacier and the cracking of ice. It was the last week of May, and the thaw had set in, so that many of the high ice pinnacles were shrinking dejectedly, and the rivulets were swollen. Through this wilderness I tramped resolutely, whistling a little obviously, my mind torn between the *yeti* and the South Col.

To my Sherpas, as we sat beside the big camp fire talking, there was never a doubt about the existence of the *yeti*. He was something they had grown up with; if you asked them whether they believed in the Snowman they answered with an air of pitying wonder, as if you had asked a London bus driver whether he believed in Tower Bridge. All had some experience to recount, and some claimed to have seen the Snowman. Several were present on a famous occasion when a *yeti* appeared on the bill above Thyangboche in the middle of a religious festival, well attended by the Sherpas; the monks, casting about for a method of getting rid of him, wisely ordered the monastery band to strike up a serenade on its drums and conchs, and in a trice the *yeti*, blocking his ears, had loped away into the snows. Others claimed that the roofs of their family houses, secured in the Alpine manner by piles of stones, had been rudely removed by marauding Snowmen. One said he had even seen a Snowman grubbing for roots in a garden. What did he look like? 'Exactly like you, sahib,' said the impudent minion, to raucous laughter from our companions. I ordered the removal of his ears, but nobody took any notice.

It was difficult, as a conscientious reporter, to sift fact from fancy in their accounts of such experiences; and often I recognized echoes of hobgoblins, Cornish gnomes, forest sprites, leprechauns, and other products of the peasant imagination.

'Come now,' I would say, 'stop being funny, and tell me exactly what this thing was like, that you say you saw eating onions on your uncle's veranda. How big was it? Bigger than you?'

'A little, sahib, a bit smaller than you, but very big *this* way. It was brown, and covered all over with hair, very rough. Sometimes it walked on all fours, and sometimes it walked upright. It made two kinds of noises. Sometimes it grunted, like this—urgh! urgh!—and sometimes it sort of whistled. It had toes, just like us. It moved very fast. It had two eyes. It had ears. It was covered all over with brown hair. It had a sort of crest of hair on its head. Oh yes, and it had its feet on backwards, sahib!'

Feet on backwards, breasts dangling so low that the female could only run uphill, arms strong enough to crush a yak, a liking for *chang*—all these picturesque details somehow detracted, I thought, from the scientific value of such accounts. But there emerged through the wild fancies, all the same, a brown, vaguely anthropomorphic figure, covered with hair, with a crested head, on which all the Sherpas seemed to agree: and coupled with this common image was a fear of the thing tinged with loathing, as if the *yeti* were evil or dirty (he must be very dirty indeed to cause the Sherpas any qualms). 'He is bad,' they would say, 'and sometimes he eats yaks, and sometimes humans, and his hair is unpleasant.' I often wondered just how bad he was, as I wandered through the moraine in search of him.

A year later, when Everest was far behind us and we had all tasted a little of the fruits of fortune, I was travelling in a train with Ed Hillary, Charles Evans, and George Lowe, between Philadelphia and Washington. It was very late at night. The Philadelphia lecture was over, and in the morning there was to be a ceremony at the White House. The train, a slow local, rocked and clattered clumsily through the night. Two elderly ladies gossiped breathily in one corner, and three men lay in another, their feet on the seats, their felt hats tipped over their eyes, snoring. Sometimes a sleepy man in a white overall wandered through, selling milk and soft drinks. The conductor sat in a window-seat puffing a big cigar.

As we chatted, Evans chanced to pull out his wallet, to find his railway ticket; and as he did so I noticed tucked away in one of its pockets a small cellophane envelope, containing what looked like a tuft of rough brown hairs. It was really none of my business, but I could not resist asking him what they were; for though Evans is a brain surgeon, it seemed an odd thing to be carrying about so close to the heart, the hairs having little in common with those sweet ribbon-bound curls sometimes to be found in the recesses of swains.

'Oh,' said he casually, idly pulling the envelope out, 'they're some hairs from the scalp of an Abominable Snowman!'

The conductor puffed away at his cigar; the three men snored; the ladies shared their sewing-circle antipathies; and we Britons, suddenly galvanized into awareness, eagerly examined this queer trophy. It was a bizarre moment. Charles, now showing more interest himself, displayed the hairs with a distinctly proprietorial air; and I rashly offered, on behalf of my newspaper, to buy them from him for examination. As we swayed over the Delaware that night it really seemed to me that we might at last have mastered the secret of the Snowman.

With infinite calm Evans told us how he had acquired the bristles. After the Everest expedition he had stayed behind in the Sherpa country to do some mapping, climbing, and exploration on his own. One night he and some Sherpas had settled for the night in a yak-herders' shelter called Thagnak, at about 16,000 feet, and the conversation had turned, as it so often did, to the *yeti*. The Sherpas made their usual muddled contribution to the discussion, all agreeing again on the general character-istics of the beast, and describing its details with inelegant variations; and in the course of the talk one of them remarked to Evans: 'Of course, you know there's a *yeti* scalp at the Buddhist temple at Pangboche?' Evans knew nothing of the kind, and was naturally excited. This might be just the kind of *yeti* trace that would settle the identity of the thing. When their survey work was finished, he and the Sherpa Da Tenzing crossed a pass and arrived at Pangboche.

'There was a little Sherpa, dressed in rags, in charge of the temple, and we asked him to show us round. When we had looked at it—it was a dark and dingy place—we asked if we could see the *yeti* scalp. He didn't object, so we climbed up the stairs to a room where they kept all the ceremonial masks and robes. Everything was very dusty and disorderly, and he couldn't find the scalp at first. We were beginning to wonder if it was there at all when at last he pulled it out and dusted it with his coat-sleeve and held it out to us.'

'Well, what was it like? Go on!'

But Evans was never to be hurried. He blew his nose with dignity, and continued: 'It was a piece of hard black skin, somewhere between a dome and a cone. If it was a scalp, it had been cut off above the ears and eyes, and on the outside of it there were stiff bristly hairs, black and chestnut, about an inch long.'

'The ones you've got!' said I.

'Wait,' said Charles. 'On each side of the cone these bristles lay flat. In some places they'd been worn away. But over the top of the cone, in a straight line, they stood up like a sort of crest. It was really very like the Sherpas' description of a Snowman's head!'

Evans had never seen a head of this shape. The nearest he
could think of was a gorilla's, which comes to less of a peak and
has softer hair. Nobody knew how the object had come to
Pangboche, though it was associated with a magician of antiq-
uity named Tsang Dorje, who was supposed to be able to fly.
When they had finished looking at the scalp, it was turned
upside-down and passed around by its keeper as the hat is
passed round, and with the same intention. As a contributor
Evans thought he was justified in pulling out a couple of hairs;
and so it happened that we were examining them in that
squeaky old American train, in that dark American night,
7,000 miles away.

As Evans said, they obviously did not come from any of the
animals known to frequent the region of Pangboche—the yak,
the wild sheep, the fox, the wolf, the musk deer, and the tail-less
rat. They were genuinely 'x', the unknown quantity, plucked
from the skin of an unnamed creature, taken by a Tibetan magician to a Buddhist temple in the shadow of Everest.

'Very interesting,' said Hillary. 'Reminds me of the time we
were crossing the pass between the Gunara and the Khumbu in
'52—remember, George? It was about 19,500. We had five
Sherpas. The side we were climbing was pretty steep, believe
you me; we were about half-way up, and I was helping two old
Sherpas who were making heavy weather of it. They both
stopped and I turned back to help them along. I found one of
them showing the other something he'd picked up off a rock. I
asked them what it was, and the chap who was holding the
thing held it out for me. It was a tuft of bristles, very coarse and
blackish, like these.

'Well, I knew they couldn't be yak hairs. It was much too
steep for yak. Anyway, the hairs were too coarse. I asked the
Sherpas what they were, and they said they were *yeti* hairs. I
tried to take the tuft—thought I'd take them triumphantly back
to civilization, you see—but the Sherpa holding them said,

"Very bad!" and he threw them over the bluff. He was obviously repelled by them. I remember the hairs especially because
they were so stiff; but I certainly wasn't going to go over the
bluff to examine them more closely. As I remember them, they
were very like these.'

Fired by these tales, the first thing I did in Washington was
to arrange for the hairs to be flown home to England. John
Hunt, in America for the White House ceremony, agreed to
take them home for me, and took charge of them with an air of
infinite responsibility, as if he were delivering the blue-print of
a hydrogen bomb. In London they were taken to the Natural
History Museum in Kensington; and they were also examined
by the Forensic Laboratory at Scotland Yard, an odd job even
for that versatile institution.

Away in America we waited with bated breath for the outcome of these examinations. The more we thought about the
hairs, the harsher and stiffer and stranger they grew: the more
mysterious in my imagination became that old Tibetan wizard,
flying through the glaciers scalping Snowmen; the more preg-
nant with significance became the scalp itself, now back in the
dust of the upstairs room, among the devil-faces, long saffron
robes, bones, and weird ritual instruments. As our tour continued, we took to visiting the local zoos, hanging over the railings
that surrounded the big bears and measuring the feet of langur
monkeys. At Central Park Zoo in New York a friendly but baffled superintendent allowed us to test the hair of an orangutan
for texture, and to inspect with a peculiar intensity of interest
the scalp of a young gorilla. The more we considered the circumstances, the more possible it seemed that we were about to
solve the mystery; and the more convinced I became that Evans
had, by these odd means, discovered the presence in the
Himalaya of some unsuspected primate (perhaps a gorilla).

But there are creatures that even the American zoos do not
show to their visitors, and holy men in India and Nepal whose

relics are evidently of dubious sanctity. Bang went my conception of the magician; back on his pedestal of mystery strode the *yeti*. In Denver, Colorado, the truth arrived in a cable from London, and a few days of high excitement degenerated into a moment of hilarity. 'All experts are of opinion,' the cable ran frigidly, 'that hairs are those of a hog repeat hog. What can you do to recover our money?'

Since then that poor scalp at Pangboche has been raided again for its bristles. A later British expedition extracted some and sent them to England. A wandering Indian scientist took some more, and had them examined at the Peabody Museum of Natural History at Yale. The poor little custodian, in his rags, must constantly be running up and down the stairs, scrabbling among the ceremonial masks: and nobody has had the heart to tell him that it is probably only the skin of a pig—perhaps not even a scalp, they say, but a bit of rump or a hog's back stretched and shaped to assume another form.

But all this was unknown to me as we sat around the fire on those pleasant May evenings, and when I peered with such nagging forebodings into the gullies of the glacier. If anyone had told me there was a *yeti* scalp at Pangboche, I would have packed a bag of potatoes and walked there overnight: for there is something obsessive and irresistible about the enigma of the Snowman.

9

Ascent

THE DAY OF THE FIRST ASSAULT came and went, and I heard over the radio one evening that Evans and Bourdillon had reached the South Summit, higher than any man had climbed before, but had fallen back to the South Col exhausted. As expected, the climb directly from Camp VIII had been too far for them; their new oxygen kit had given them trouble; they had stood upon that little bump I had noticed from Pumori, only 500 feet below the summit, and after seeing something of the cruel final ridge had withdrawn to the Col.

Now there approached the moment of the second assault, the more powerful of the two. Hillary and Tenzing would have many advantages. The weather was fine for them, and the snow that still fell on Base Camp each evening petered out two thousand feet above us. They would have a last camp, pitched at 27,900 feet, from which to make the final spring to the summit. Their oxygen equipment had been thoroughly proved. They were fit as fiddles still, and greatly encouraged by what Evans and Bourdillon had achieved. If it helped at all, the good wishes of the world by now went with them (for over the months, what with Hunt's frequent authoritative messages, my own dispatches, and the incredible potpourri of misinformation that emanated from Katmandu, a public beyond the dreams—or nightmares— of the old Everesters now had its eyes glued greedily on the mountain).

May 29 was the chosen day. On the evening of the 28th I had as my companion at Base Camp Griffith Pugh, the physiologist, and we sat late beside the fire drinking and talking, while he puffed at an odd angular French pipe. I always enjoyed his company. He was full of peculiar knowledge, and passed it on at surprising moments in a hesitating, slow-spoken, pipe-puffing manner; as if some gentle country parson, settling down for a quiet scriptural chat with his parishioners, were suddenly to present some theories about Kafka, the dipping hem-line, or space travel. That night, I remember, we did in fact discuss religion, or at least those activities, such as yoga and Moral Re-Armament, which leap and linger around the fringes of it.

At last, when the fire began to die and the cold night air came creeping chillingly up the glacier, we arose and stretched and moved towards our tents.

'Are you coming up the mountain again tomorrow?' he said. 'I'm moving off about eight, if you'd like to come with me.' I said I had not planned a climb, because I thought I should stay near my communications for the final news, and I was afraid some of our competitors might arrive at Base Camp at the crucial moment.

'I think you're wrong,' said Dr. Pugh. 'I think you ought to be up in the Cwm when they come back from the assault. What if somebody does arrive here? You'll be bringing the news down yourself, so they can hardly get hold of it before you do.'

It was the radio transmitters I was thinking of, and the havoc they could wreak with all our well-laid plans; but he convinced me, and before I went to bed I untangled my crampons and made sure that my ice-axe was still standing, an esoteric talisman, in the snow outside my tent. As I sank into my sleeping-bag, I sleepily considered my situation. I would certainly hear of the ascent of Everest, or the failure of the attempt, before any other correspondent. I had runners at Base Camp who would get my news back to Katmandu in six or seven days. There the ambassador was ready to send a brief message over his radio to London. I reckoned that a message sent in code by this means would be in the newspaper eight days after the event.

But there was always the radio at Namche Bazar. There was a risk attached to its use, for a message might easily go astray, or somehow leak out and be miraculously deciphered by these many correspondents who hung about the Indian Embassy in Katmandu: but it would get my news to London in a matter of hours, a marvellous possibility. I fumbled about in my baggage in the dark, and extracted that new and nasty code whose key, I knew, was safe in Katmandu. How did it go? *Message to begin: Snow Conditions Bad.* Oh Mr. Tiwari, I hope you will both help me and forgive me! Remember all those aspirins I gave you!

'We'll go straight up to Camp III,' said Pugh as we tramped away to the foot of the icefall. 'Nobody uses Camp II nowadays, it's unnecessary anyway and it's getting to look rather dangerous. You'll see some big changes in the icefall.'

And indeed I did. Gone was the track intermittently visible between the snowfalls, a week or two before. The whole messy crumbling cataract was messier and crumblier than ever before, for the summer heat had melted many of its huge *seracs*, widened its crevasses, and made its ice-bridges soggy and ominous. Michael Westmacott had been working inside this horrible place for ten days, keeping some kind of route open, so that the climbers in the Western Cwm would not find, when it was time to descend, that they had been trapped up there by its slow and sticky disintegration. Here and there were signs of his work, and I could picture him vividly working there alone, with a silent Sherpa to belay him, cutting steps, fixing ropes, moving ladders, all in the white empty wilderness of the ice. In one place a crevasse had widened so severely that he had lashed a couple of poles to the aluminium ladder that bridged it. Elsewhere, jumping and scrambling among the pinnacles, he had cut away dangerous and tottering *seracs*, hammered in pitons, and tried to discipline those little red flags which, egged on by the thaw, persisted in sliding away from the route. I have often thought of Westmacott since, immured there in the icefall, and marvelled at his tenacity.

We climbed slowly. Now and then we exchanged a few words, but for most of the time I thought about our adventure, and wondered what was happening at that very moment, in the middle of the morning, May 29, 9,000 feet above us. You could see nothing from the icefall, except the empty valley behind you and an occasional ridge of the soaring rock walls that hemmed it in; and on such a day one felt blind and helpless shut in there. We stopped at Camp II for some lemonade and boiled sweets. The two tents were still there, muckier and more forlorn than they used to be, but a huge decaying tower of ice seemed about to fall with a clatter on top of them, and just beside the camp a big insidious crevasse had split the small plateau as a wedge splits a stone. No longer did we have to boil the snow to get some water. The Sherpas took our mugs and, striding off across the snow, came to a little glacier puddle, a gift from the thaw. Camp II was an ignored and abandoned place; whatever happened on the mountain, our expedition already had a dying fall. Hunt had plans for a third assault, but I suspected that most of the climbers were as tired as those two small wind-blown tents appeared to be.

The afternoon came, free of snow, and we pushed into the upper part of the icefall. This was an entirely new landscape to me, as if some petulant child, tired of his sand castle, had kicked it about with his tiny feet and made a different kind of slobber out of it. After an hour of climbing we came across a sharp straight gully, running downwards parallel to the route we were following. Suddenly I heard from the top of the gully a rumbling, roaring, clattering noise; and there rolled by us an avalanche of ice, snow, and stones. Pugh and I threw ourselves hastily to the ground; but it swept past us imperiously, with never a glance in our direction, down through the ice-castles and the leaning blocks, with a noise like the passage of a million marbles, until the last stone and the last lump of ice had rattled away out of sight and hearing. We picked up our axes and our rucksacks, and continued our journey wearily.

Camp III, as the evening arrived, with a few wisps of snow, no more, and a glorious sunset colouring the face of Lhotse far ahead of us: I walked through the snow to a little plateau outside the camp, overlooking the valley below us. There the icefall crawled down the mountain-side, huge and shapeless in the dusk, and Pumori and its sisters stood in shadow above the glacier. Far down the hill ran the Khumbu between its mountain walls, twisting a little, like a crumpled ribbon, but marching steadfastly to Thyangboche. That was the way my news must go, down the green and into the blue. It was all dark and deserted; for the first time since I had come to Everest, I felt lonely looking at it, and wished there were a few lights twinkling down there, with a warm fire-side below mountain meadows, or an English inn, with tankards, chicken, old waiters in frayed tail-coats, prints of forgotten horses, and trout for breakfast. Now that the adventure was approaching its last climax Everest felt an especially aloof and unfriendly place, a blind thing that took no notice of us, but simply went its senseless seasonal way—snows and sunshine, heat and cold, thaw and monsoon—like some mindless robot, deposited to tick away in silence in an empty corner of the world.

I shivered, and kicked myself for morbidity, and returned to camp.

So at last to Camp IV again, out of the cruel white desert of snow. The tension and suppressed emotion that now filled this camp emanated from it like ripples, so that far down the Cwm, when the tents first appeared as blobs on a distant ridge, a sharp tang of expectancy suddenly struck us. It was midday, and most of the climbers were gathered there. The months had left their mark on them, as on the mountain itself. I remembered them all as I first saw them, at the end of March: Evans, Gregory, and Bourdillon at Thyangboche; the New Zealanders crawling out of their tents at Lake Camp; Band, Ward, and Westmacott, cheerfully hauling me up the icefall; Noyce, Wylie, Stobart, and Pugh, in the big dome tent at Base Camp; Hunt himself, the leader, cream-faced at Lobuje. They were gay and friendly still, but indelibly marked by the strains of the campaign. Evans and Bourdillon, fresh from 28,500 feet, were visibly weakened by their *tour de force*. Bourdillon's huge, graceful frame looked shrunken; Evans, beneath the queer half-beard dictated by his oxygen equipment, looked a great deal less rubicund than he had a month or two before (and infinitely less Dickensian, in every way, than he was to look in future months over a port and a good cigar at many a London dining table). Even Alfred Gregory, sharpest and liveliest of men, was moving a little slower than usual, and his incisive Lancashire voice had lost some of its edge. Westmacott was there, in his wide bush hat; George Band, tall and sprawling still, who was later to stand upon the summit of Kanchenjunga; Stobart with his camera; and a cheerful company of Sherpas, many of them fresh from the South Col, and proud of the fact.

And there in his shanty-tent was Hunt, still hideous with ointment; a heroic figure, I thought, like some grizzled Hannibal in climbing-boots, awaiting the arrival of the elephants. This was nearly the end of the adventure. Soon, within an hour or two, we would know whether all his careful plans had succeeded, whether his own wonderful climb to 28,000 feet had been justified, whether the loading tables had been correct, the choice of climbers wise; whether the weather he had trusted had turned sour on him, whether the equipment he had chosen had proved sound; or whether, when Hillary and Tenzing returned defeated from the last ridge of Everest, he would have to begin all over again, threading his teams of porters through the dangers of the icefall, computing his tables again, naming his teams, and preparing (as he had planned) for the third assault which he himself would lead, come what may. He had given Hillary a small white crucifix to place upon the summit of Everest, if he reached it; if Hillary did not get there, Hunt would place it on the top himself.

I joined him in the shade, and ate thirteen more of the Swiss biscuits.

'Well, dear old James,' he said. 'It's nearly over now, I suppose. Supposing they climbed it, now, how soon d'you think you could get the news home to England? A week? Or less?'

I told him I thought I might get a brief message back to London rather quicker than that, if all went well; and a longer account of Hillary's and Tenzing's climb, well, yes, about a week.

'Of course it would be marvellous,' said I, 'if we could get it back to London in time for the Coronation, wouldn't it? Let me see, May 30 today. Coronation Day is June 2. Thirty days have September, April, June, and. . . . Three days, really, counting today. I suppose it's just possible, John, but don't count on it. What do you think, it would be rather good, wouldn't it?'

But he was listening to me no longer. Tilting back in his canvas chair, like a rather unorthodox Hollywood director giving instructions to the gantry camera, he was looking through his binoculars at the Lhotse Face in front of us. I looked hard through mine, but could see nothing, only the endless mass of ice-blocks, rumpled *seracs*, and snow.

'There they are!' someone shouted. 'There! Just behind that big *serac!* See them? You know the one, Charles, that brute of a thing with, the big crevasses just behind it. See them? There they go! Just crossing the gap!'

I looked again, and high, high on the face of the mountain sure enough, there they were. Five little figures were moving slowly down the snow: Hillary, Tenzing, Lowe, Noyce, and the remarkable Sherpa Pasang Phutar. How were they walking? Jauntily, like men who have reached a summit? Or dragging their feet in the depression of failure? Nobody could tell, for they were just specks on a mountain wall.

What a day it was for great news! That old secluded valley of the Cwm was crisp and sparkling, like a girl decked out in a party frock. The sky was a miraculous blue, the floor of the Cwm dazzlingly white. The massive wall of Nuptse, bounding the Cwm on its southern side, shone mysteriously like silk or rubbed velvet, with the curious greasy sheen of melting snow. From the ridge of Lhotse, directly above us, a small spiral of snow eddied and swirled into the sky, like a genie released from a bottle. There was little wind, and we sat there becalmed in the stillness and the sunshine. The Cwm was silent, as always; but sometimes we heard a sudden high-pitched whistle, thrilling and menacing, as a boulder screamed down from the heights above.

The hours dragged by. Endlessly we discussed the chances of success. Hillary and Tenzing had been seen at nine o'clock the day before crossing the South Summit and going strongly up the ridge. With the rest of the morning before them, they had plenty of time to reach the top and return; but who knew what that last ridge was like? It showed in some of the aerial pictures, but not very clearly; perhaps there was some insuperable obstacle along it, an impassable ledge, dangerous cornices; perhaps their oxygen had failed them, in the last 500 feet; perhaps, faced with the horrors of the altitude, their will had faltered or their bodies slumped. We sat in the dome tent and talked about it.

'Just coming down to Camp VI,' said the watchers outside. 'Somebody's sitting down, can't make out who. Anyone care to lay the odds?'

They were clearer now, those little figures on the mountainside. At least they were all safe, I thought. No need for my catastrophe codes, nor my prepared obituaries. Once they were down in the Cwm there was only the passage of the icefall to worry about; and exhausted though the climbers were, I thought they would probably survive that. Not a broken limb had the party suffered; only colds, stomach upsets, and a few minor cases of frost-bite.

Inside the tent there was a mess of newspapers: *The Times*, the *Auckland Weekly News*, with an enormous picture of a lady in a picture hat, a big bouquet pinned to her bosom, presenting prizes, presiding at a banquet, marrying her daughter off, being introduced to a duchess, or performing some such immemorial social duty. I remembered Roberts's description of his first arrival in New Zealand, when the woman in black behind the hotel reception desk raised her thin eyebrows at his open shirt, and pursed her tight lips primly when he asked the way to the bar. It seemed a strange and bourgeois society for heroes to come from, and I found it difficult to equate the lady in her blue crepe with her countrymen up there on the heights, swaggering, big and breezy.

'Well, yes' (I heard a snatch of conversation through the open door of the tent). 'I suppose so, but the moon will never be quite the same. Who cares about the moon? There are no *little* moons to start with. Nobody goes exploring moons at week-ends, like we go climbing mountains. Anyway, you can keep the moon so far as I'm concerned. All I'm interested in is creature comforts. A l-o-n-g glass of beer! A really good steak! Or a good fug at the Climbers' Club Hut at Helyg!'

Hastily I turned and crumpled the pages of my newspaper. Somebody had been doing *The Times* crossword puzzle, with a muffled stub of red crayon.

26 *Foot—foot—foot—foot—slogging over—*
(Kipling) (6).

The red crayon had answered that one in bold and confident letters, so bold that it had gone through the paper, and I could see where the crossword puzzler, on some cold and lonely evening in a flapping tent, had folded the newspaper to give himself something solid to write on. Who had it been, I wondered? Westmacott, during his icefall vigil? Noyce, in some high camp on the Lhotse Face? Hunt, breaking himself away for a moment from the perpetual preoccupations of leadership?

Here was a dispatch of mine. 'Plans For Double Assault On Peak Of Everest'. Somewhere between the mountain and the printed page the wrong dateline had crept into it. I had sent the message from Camp III, but it was headed 'Base Camp, Everest'. 'This is a bleak spot high above the Khumbu Glacier,' I was alleged to have written of our little Base Camp on the Khumbu Glacier, 'with the ugly mass of the icefall spilling below.' Oh well, probably nobody noticed; to most newspaper readers, Base Camp, Everest, was practically the South Summit. 'Oh my goodness me,' they would say to me in America, 'all those weeks on the glacier! Didn't you feel giddy?'

There was a kind of feverish hush over the camp now, and John Hunt sat outside his tent on a packing-case, his waterproof hat jammed on his head, as tense as a violin string. I could see the little figures no longer. They had left the Lhotse Face, and were hidden behind a ridge at the top end of the Cwm. They must be going well, to get there so soon. Would they move so swiftly if they were suffering the pangs of defeat? On the other hand, *could* they move so swiftly if they had reached the summit of Everest? I remembered the terrible exhaustion of the old Everest climbers, and wondered if a man could go so well after a night at 27,800 feet.

There was a clatter of crampons outside, and Tom Stobart stumped off up the valley with his camera to meet the summit party. I watched him labouring away along the snow, a lonely but determined figure, until he vanished over a ridge. All was then empty in the Cwm around us. The face of Lhotse was blank and lifeless, and all we could see stretching away to its foot was the rolling empty snow. Somewhere hidden away there, not so very far from us, were Hillary, Tenzing, and their support party. It was one o'clock, but nobody felt like lunch.

In the corner of the tent there was a radio receiver, tilting drunkenly on the edge of a cardboard box. As the minutes lurched past it murmured intermittent music, and then a cultured Indian voice announced that this was All-India Radio, and that here was the news. We pricked up our ears. Sure enough, very soon Everest was mentioned. Agency messages had now confirmed, said the radio, that the British assault on Everest had failed, and that the expedition was withdrawing from the mountain. There go my competitors, I thought, as active as ever. A slight communal guffaw ran around the tent. Somebody twiddled the knob, half-amused, half-irritated, and:

'There they are!'

I rushed to the door of the tent, and there emerging from a little gully, not more than five hundred yards away, were four worn figures in windproof clothing. As a man we leapt out of the camp and up the slope, our boots sinking and skidding in the soft snow, Hunt wearing big dark snow-goggles, Gregory with the bobble on the top of his cap jiggling as he ran, Bourdillon with braces outside his shirt, Evans with the rim of his hat turned up in front like an American stevedore's. Wildly we ran and slithered up the snow, and the Sherpas, emerging excitedly from their tents, ran after us.

I could not see the returning climbers very clearly, for the exertion of running had steamed up my goggles, so that I looked ahead through a thick mist. But I watched them approaching dimly, with never a sign of success or failure, like drugged men. Down they tramped, mechanically, and up we raced, trembling with expectation. Soon I could not see a thing for the steam, so I pushed the goggles up from my eyes; and just as I recovered from the sudden dazzle of the snow I caught sight of George Lowe, leading the party down the hill. He was raising his arm and waving as he walked! It was thumbs up! Everest was climbed! Hillary brandished his ice-axe in weary triumph; Tenzing slipped suddenly sideways, recovered, and shot us a brilliant white smile; and they were among us, back from the summit, with men pumping their hands and embracing them, laughing, smiling, crying, taking photographs, laughing again, crying again, till the noise and the delight of it all rang down the Cwm and set the Sherpas, following us up the hill, laughing in anticipation.

Down we went again, Hillary and Tenzing still roped together, Tom Bourdillon rolling back with his hands in his pockets, grinning, Gregory, fired by the occasion, already sharp and vigorous again. Above the camp most of the Sherpas were waiting in an excited smiling group. As the greatest of their little race approached them they stepped out, one by one, to congratulate him. Tenzing received them like a modest prince. Some bent their bodies forward, their hands clasped as if in prayer. Some shook hands lightly and delicately, the fingers scarcely touching. One old veteran, his black twisted pig-tail flowing behind him, bowed gravely to touch Tenzing's hand with his forehead; just as Sonam, down in the valley, had touched the likeness of that saintly abbot.

We moved into the big dome tent, and sat around the summit party, throwing questions at them, still laughing, unable to believe the truth. Everest was climbed, and these two mortal men in front of us, sitting on old boxes, had stood upon its summit, the highest place on earth! And nobody knew but us! The day was still dazzlingly bright—the snow so white, the sky so blue; and the air was still so vibrant with excitement; and the news, however much we expected it, was still somehow such a wonderful surprise—shock waves of that moment must still linger there in the Western Cwm, so potent were they, and so gloriously charged with pleasure. Now and then the flushed face of a Sherpa appeared in the doorway with a word of delight; and as we lay there on boxes, rolls of bedding, and sleeping-bags, Hillary and Tenzing ate a leathery omelette apiece, and told us their story. I can hear Hillary's voice today, and see the lump of omelette protruding inside his left cheek, as he paused for a moment from mastication to describe the summit of Mount Everest.

The whole world knows the story now: how the two of them had spent a terrible night in the tiny tent of Camp IX, crookedly pitched on an uncomfortable ridge, one half of the floor higher than the other; how they had struggled and talked and dreamed the night away, eating sardines; how early on the morning of May 29 they had crept out of the tent, to find the day fine and clear, so that Thyangboche monastery could be seen there, ten miles away and 19,000 feet below, and the little lake, tucked away below Pumori, that Sonam and I had visited two months before; how they had laboured along the last ridge, and hauled themselves up a brutal chimney, and expected each successive bump to be the summit; until at last, at 11:30 in the morning, they had found themselves truly at the top, with the flags they carried fluttering in the breeze.

Hillary had planted John's crucifix, as he had promised, and Tenzing had placed some small offerings on the ground, to propitiate the divinities supposed to live upon that Himalayan Olympus. They had embraced each other, and taken photographs, and eaten some mint cake; and after fifteen minutes on the summit, they had turned and begun the downward climb.

'What did it feel like when we got there? Well I'll tell you, though I don't know if Tenzing agrees; when we found it really was the summit at last I heaved a sigh of relief, and that's a fact. No more steps to cut! No more ridges to traverse! It was a great relief to me, I can tell you. D'you agree, Tenzing?'

And Tenzing, his hat pushed back on his head, his face permanently wreathed and crinkled with smiles, laughed and nodded and ate his omelette, while the worshipping Sherpas at the door gazed at him like apostates before the Pope. Indeed, he was a fine sight, sitting there in his moment of triumph, before the jackals of fame closed in upon him.

'Yes, but there must have been more than mere relief in your mind,' I said to him, 'after all these years of Everest climbing. What else did you feel when you stood upon the summit?'

This time Tenzing paused in his eating and thought hard about his reply. 'Very excited,' he said judicially, 'not too tired, very pleased.'

10

Descent

HALF PAST TWO on the afternoon of May 30. I scribbled it all down in a tattered old notebook, drinking in the flavour of the occasion, basking in the aura of incredulous delight that now flooded through our little camp. The talk was endless and vivacious, and would no doubt continue throughout that long summer afternoon and into the night; but there were only three full days to the Coronation, and as I scribbled I realized that I must start down the mountain again that very afternoon, to get a message off to Namche the next morning. This time there would be no night's rest at Camp III. I must go straight down the icefall to Base Camp that evening. My body, still aching from the upward climb in the morning, did not like the sound of this at all; but at the back of my slightly befuddled brain a small voice told me that there could be no argument. Wilfrid Noyce had always planned to make this last dash down the mountain-side for me; but now I was here myself, and need not bother him.

'I'll come with you, James!' said Michael Westmacott instantly, when I told them my plans; and remembering the newly oozing ice-bog of the route, I accepted his offer gratefully. We loaded our rucksacks, fastened our crampons, shook hands all round, and set off down the slope. 'Good luck!' a voice called from the dome tent; I turned around to wave my thanks, and stood for a moment (till the rope tugged me on) looking at the blank face of Lhotse, just falling into shadow, and the little clump of happy tents that was Camp IV. Christmas angels were in the Cwm that day.

So we strode off together down the valley. In a downhill climb the most experienced man should travel last; but I was so obviously in a condition of impending disintegration, and the way was so sticky and unpleasant from the thaw, that Westmacott went first, and I followed. At the head of the Cwm, though we did not know it, Wilfrid Noyce, Charles Wylie, and some Sherpas were making their way down to Camp IV from the Lhotse Face, where they had been packing up the tents to bring them lower. As they crossed a small ridge they caught sight of our two small figures, far below, all alone in the Cwm and travelling hard towards Camp III. Perhaps there were ghosts about, Noyce thought as he watched our dour, silent progress; the angel theory did not occur to him.

For me it was a wet and floundering march. So soft, receptive, and greedy was the snow that at almost every step I sank deeply into it, often up to my thighs, and had then to extricate myself with infinite trouble, with that confounded rope (connecting me with Westmacott) rapidly getting tauter as I struggled, until suddenly there would be a great sharp pull upon it, and Mike would turn round to see what was happening, and find me sprawling and flapping in the snow, like some tiresome sea-creature on the sand. I remember vividly the labour and the discomfort of it all, with the wet seeping into my boots, and the shaft of my ice-axe sinking into the snow, my head heavy and my brain muzzy but excited. As we travelled down the Cwm, so the sun went down, and the valley was plunged into shadow, chilling and unfriendly.

Here and there were our footsteps of the morning's journey, barely recognizable now, but squashy and distorted, as if Snowmen had passed that way. Long and deep were the crevasses that evening, and as we crossed them their cool interiors seemed almost inviting in their placidity. The shadows chased us down the valley, and soon I could no longer watch my own image on the snow, elongated like a dream figure, with my old hat swollen on my head and my ice-axe, like a friar's stave, swinging in my hand. Before long we were peering ahead through the dusk, still struggling and slipping, but still moving steadily down the mountain.

Camp III again, in the half-light. We stopped for lemonade and sweets, and I looked about me with a sudden pang of regret at the melting plateau, the sagging tents, the tottering wireless aerial, the odd boxes and packing-cases. I would never set foot on this place again: this was my good-bye to the mountain. So befuddled was I by the altitude and the exertion, so feverish of emotion, that a hot tear came to my eye as I sat there shivering in the cold, my boots soggy and my head throbbing, looking about me at the loathsome, decaying wilderness of ice that surrounded us.

Down we plunged into the icefall, and I realized again what an odious place it had become. The bigness and messiness and cruelty of it all weighed heavily upon me, a most depressing sensation. Any grandeur the icefall possessed had gone, and squalidness had overcome it. Now more than ever it was a moving thing; *seracs* were disintegrating, plateaus splitting, ice-towers visibly melting; and there were creaking, groaning, and cracking noises.

> *The ice was here, the ice was there,*
> *The ice was all around;*
> *It cracked and growled, and roared and howled,*
> *Like noises in a swound!*

Through this pile of white muck we sped, and as we travelled I wondered (in a hazy sort of way) what we would find at the bottom. How many Izzards or Jacksons had encamped at Base Camp in my absence, setting up their transmitters, poised to fall upon the descending Sherpas? Was there any conceivable way in which the news of the ascent could have reached the glacier already? Nobody had preceded us down the mountain, but what about telepathy, mystic links, smoke signals, choughs, spiders, swounds? What if I arrived at camp to find that my news was already on its way to London and some eager Fleet Street office? I shuddered at the thought, and taking a moment off to hitch up my rucksack, nearly fell headlong into a crevasse.

'Stay where you are,' said Westmacott a little sharply. 'And belay me if you can!'

One of his pole-bridges, across a yawning chasm, had been loosened by the thaw, and looked horribly unsafe. I thrust my ice-axe into the snow and put the rope around it while Westmacott gently edged himself across. I could just see him there in the gloom, precariously balanced. One pole was lashed to another, and he had to move them around, or tie them again, or turn them over, or hitch them up, or do something or other to ensure that we were not precipitated into the depths, as Peacock once remarked, in the smallest possible fraction of the infinite divisibility of time. This, after a few anxious and shivery moments, he did: and I followed him cautiously across the void.

Who would have thought, when Hunt accepted me over that admirable lunch at the Garrick Club, that my assignment would end like this, scrambling dizzily and feverishly down the icefall of Everest in the growing darkness? Who could have supposed that I would ever find myself in quite so historically romantic a situation, dashing down the flanks of the greatest of mountains to deliver a message for the Coronation of Queen Elizabeth II? It was all perfectly—*oops, steady, nasty slippery bit!*—all perfectly ridiculous. It must all be some midnight dream, by brandy out of Gruyere; or a wild boyhood speculation, projected by some intricate mechanism of the time-space theory. Slithering down the mountain with the news from Everest! What poppycock!

'Do try and wake up,' said Westmacott. 'It would be a help if you'd belay me sometimes!'

I murmured my apologies, blushing in the dark. Indeed by now, as we passed the tents of Camp II, I was a pitiful passenger. All the pieces of equipment fastened to my person seemed to be coming undone. The ice-axe constantly slipped from my fingers and had to be picked up. The rope threatened to unloose itself. The laces of my boots trailed. The fastening of one of my crampons had broken, so that the thing was half-on, half-off my foot, and kept tripping me up. I had torn my windproof jacket on an ice-spur, and a big flap of its red material kept blowing about me in the wind. My rucksack, heavy with kit, had slipped on its harness, so that it now bumped uncomfortably about in the small of my back. (I have had similar sensations since, in less atrocious degree; for example at airports when, standing there helpless beside the gate, passport in one hand, luggage tickets in the other, mackintosh over one arm, hold-all over the right, a camera around my neck, a book under my arm, a typewriter between my knees, a ticket between my teeth—when, standing there in this clustered condition, I have been asked by some unspeakable official for my inoculation certificate.)

Still we went on, my footsteps growing slower and wearier and more fumbling, and even Westmacott rather tired by now.

Presently we made out the black murk that was the valley of the Khumbu; and shortly afterwards we lost our way. Everything had changed so in the thaw. Nothing was familiar. The little red route flags were useless. There was no sign of a track. We stood baffled for a few moments, faced with an empty, desert-like snow plateau, almost at the foot of the icefall. Then: 'Come on,' said Westmacott boldly, 'we'll try this way! We'll glissade down this slope here!'

He launched himself upon the slope, skidding down with a slithery crunching noise. I followed him at once, and, unable to avoid a hard ice-block at the bottom, stubbed my toe so violently that my big toe-nail came off. The agony of it! It was like something in an old Hollywood comedy, with indignity piled upon indignity, and the poor comic hero all but obliterated by misfortune!

But I had little time to brood upon it, for Westmacott was away again already, and the rope was pulling at me. As we neared the bottom of the icefall, the nature of the ground became even more distasteful. The little glacier rivulets which had run through this section had become swift-flowing torrents. Sometimes we balanced our shaky way along the edge of them; sometimes we jumped across; sometimes, willy-nilly, we waded through the chill water, which eddied into our boots and made them squelch as we walked.

At last, at the beginning of the glacier moraine, I thought I would not go farther. It was pitch black by now, and Westmacott was no more than a suggestion in front of me. I sat down on a boulder, panting and distraught, and disregarded the sudden sharp pull of the rope (like totally ignoring a bite on a deep-sea fishing line).

'What's the matter?'

'I think I'm going to stop here for a bit' (as casually as I could manage it) 'and get my breath back. I'll just sit here quietly for a minute or two. You go on, Mike, don't bother about me.'

There was a slight pause at the other end of the rope.

'Don't be so ridiculous,' said Westmacott: and so definitive was this pronouncement that I heaved myself to my feet again and followed him down the glacier. Indeed, we were almost there. The ground was familiar again, and above us loomed the neighbourly silhouette of Pumori. The icefall was a jumbled dream behind us. I felt in the pocket of my windproof to make sure my notes were there, with the little typed code I was going to use. All was safe.

Presently there was a bobbing light in front of us; and out of the gloom appeared an elderly Sherpa with a lantern, grinning at us through the darkness. He helped us off with our crampons and took the ice-axe from my hand, which was unaccountably shaking with the exertion.

'Anybody arrived at Base Camp?' I asked him quickly, thinking of those transmitters. 'Is Mr. Jackson here again, or Mr. Tiwari?'

'Nobody, sahib,' he replied. 'There's nobody here but us Sherpas. How are things on the mountain, sahib? Is all well up there?'

All well, I told him, shaking his good old hand. All very well.

So we plunged into our tents. There were some letters, and some newspapers, and a hot meal soon appeared. Mike came to join me in eating it, and we squeezed into my tent comfortably, and ate and read there in the warm. I was exhausted, for the climb from III to IV and thence down to base was no easy day's excursion for a beginner; and it seemed to me that the icefall, in its present debased and degenerate condition, had been nothing short of nightmarish.

'Was it really as bad as all that?' I asked. 'Or was it just me?'

'It was bad!' Westmacott replied shortly, peering at me benevolently over his spectacles, like a scholarly physician prescribing some good old-fashioned potion.

We lay and lazed there for a time, and chatted about it, and remembered now and then that Everest had been climbed, and wondered how the news would be received in London. I made a few tentative conjectures about honours lists. 'Sir Edmund Hillary' certainly sounded odd. What about Tenzing? 'Sir Tenzing and Lady Norkay'? 'Lord Norkay of Chomolungma'? But no, he was Indian, or Nepalese (nobody quite knew which), and could qualify for no such resplendent titles: he would be honoured royally anyway. We heaved a few sleepy sighs of satisfaction, and presently Westmacott eased himself gradually out of the tent. I thanked him for all his kindness on the icefall, and we said good-night. Before I could go to sleep, though, I had a job to do. Leaning over in my sleeping-bag with infinite discomfort, for my legs were as stiff as ramrods and patches of sunburn on various parts of my body made movement very painful, I extracted my typewriter from a pile of clothing and propped it on my knees to write a message. This was that brief dispatch of victory I had dreamed about through the months. Oh Mr. Tiwari at Namche and Mr. Summerhayes at Katmandu! Oh you watchful radio men in Whitehall! Oh telephone operators, typists and sub-editors, readers, listeners, statesmen, generals, presidents, kings, queens, and archbishops! I have a message for you!

Now then, let me see. Pull out the crumpled paper code; turn up the flickering hurricane lamp, it's getting dark in here; paper in the typewriter, don't bother with a carbon; prop up your legs with an old kit-bag stuffed with sweaters and socks; choose your words with a dirty broken-nailed finger; and here goes!

Snow conditions bad stop advanced base abandoned yesterday stop awaiting improvement

Which being interpreted would mean:

Summit of Everest reached on May 29 by Hillary and Tenzing.

I checked it for accuracy. Everything was right. I checked it again. Everything was still right. I took it out of the typewriter and began to fold it up to place it in its envelopes: but as I did so, I thought the words over, and recalled the wonder and delight of the occasion, and remembered that dear old Sherpa who had greeted us with his lantern, an hour or two before, when we had fallen out of the icefall.

All well! I added to the bottom of my message.

'Take this envelope to the Indians at Namche!' I said to the runner, a lanky young man with a long face, notably fast and reliable. 'Go by yourself, be swift and silent! Talk to nobody on the way! Hand it to the Indian sahib, and then run on to Chaunrikharka. Here is half your fee. The other half I will give you in Chaunrikharka. All right? Good-bye then, and good luck! Mind you are both swift and silent!'

I watched him leave the camp, and wave his farewell from the distant ridge, and disappear down the glacier. One more task I must do that morning, before I followed him with all possible speed, to meet him on the other side of Namche and make sure that all had gone well. If the Indians declined to send the message, I must go and see them myself and try to persuade them: but I would rather avoid the village, in case they asked me awkward questions about the nature of my message, or the reason for my departure from the mountain. And first I must send a message by the normal route, over the hills to Katmandu. If the radio failed me, the news would still reach London in a week, as I had promised John in the Western Cwm.

I hammered it out on my typewriter in the morning sunshine, from the notes I had scribbled at Camp IV the day before. It all came quickly and easily, so fresh and vivid was the experience, so glittering the news, and so excited was I by what I had seen. Yesterday, high in the Cwm, this excitement had been blunted a little by the altitude; today, though my body was aching still, it all came flooding over me with a new stimulation. I banged it out fast, only occasionally delayed when the wind caught a sheet of paper and sent it flying helter-skelter across the moraine, chased by a few laughing Sherpas, frying-pans in hand. Soon it was finished, and sealing it thoroughly in three envelopes, I gave it to the last of my runners. All the others were out, somewhere in the mountains between Everest and Katmandu; but I had saved the best of them for these last dispatches.

They bowed, shook hands, plunged the dispatches into their cloaks, and left. I would meet them on the road back to the capital, when they were returning to Sola Katmandu, their job finished; but I knew them well and trusted them, and I paid them the whole of their fee in advance, together with that handsome bonus reserved for those who did it in six days. Sure enough, they performed their promise exactly, and I next saw them (only to say good-bye) on a misty grassy ridge half-way to Katmandu.

Base Camp was almost deserted. There were only Westmacott, a few Sherpas, and I. Some of the other climbers might get down there that evening: the rest, conscientiously packing up some gear in the Cwm, would return the next day. I packed my various bags, threw away the rubbish, and distributed my loads among the Sherpas. The treasure chests were much lighter now, and I had lost a few of my possessions: but I had acquired a minute pair of Tibetan boots, made at Namche for my elder son and sent to me as a gift from Roberts, who had commissioned them on his way south. For the rest, my goods, like myself, were a great deal shabbier, more tattered, dirtier, and more threadbare than they had been when I set out with such lively confidence from Katmandu.

I had an early lunch (boiled potatoes, chocolate, cheese, and lemonade), shook hands with Mike, hoisted my rucksack on my back, and left the camp. I planned to reach Lobuje that night, and to continue the next day into the valley of the Dudh Khosi, south of Namche. In the old days this was four or five days' march, but it was important to me to get to the other side of Namche as quickly as possible—the runner would probably hand my message to the Indians on the following morning. So we marched off down the glacier at good speed. I looked back once, not to see Everest again, but only to wave good-bye to Westmacott, still sitting in his wide hat on a packing-case in the camp, reading *The Times*. Very soon the mountain was behind us, and we were threading our way through the dozens of streams, pools, and waterfalls that now, under the impact of summer, watered the moraine. I walked in a semi-daze, numbed by excitement and exertion, thinking dimly and pleasantly of far-away places.

We passed Lake Camp without a halt. Its sheet of water was still grey and forbidding, and there were a few piles of burnt sticks and ashes which showed where the hardy Sherpas had sheltered from the blizzard all those weeks before. Sonam, marching beside me, touched my shoulder and pointed behind us to the distant ridge, on the flank of Pumori, where we had sat and eaten our snow sandwiches and gazed in wonder into the Western Cwm. If we climbed there again, I thought, there would still be nothing to see on Everest; the flags on the summit would be indistinguishable, if they were not already blown down by the wind, and only the eye of faith could see John's little crucifix in the snow. Sonam smiled gently and, for no particular reason, reached out as we walked and shook my hand.

So we came to Lobuje, a green and pleasant place. A little stream ran beside the yak-herders' hut we slept in, and the grass outside was speckled with flowers. There were signs of recent occupation inside, for during the expedition most of the climbers had come down here, at one time or another, for a rest; and here Tom Stobart, wheezing and panting in the darkness of the hut, had weathered his attack of pneumonia. Evening fell soon after we reached the place, and we sat late around the fire eating potatoes and talking about *yetis*. By now, with the messages away, I had told all that faithful little company about the ascent of Everest, and we drank our *chang* as a libation.

I woke early next morning, and, putting in train a cup of tea and some breakfast, strolled off into a neighbouring rock gully which would have led me, had I the time or the inclination to follow it, into the neighbouring valley of the Chola Kola. It was one of those still, oppressive, grey, sinister Snowmen gullies, and I did not go far along it. No Snowmen were in sight; but when I climbed upon a little rock platform beside it, I saw away up the glacier, coming down from Everest, a solitary figure. My heart bounded. Could it be that some wretched Sherpa had sold his soul to the press, had hastened down from the Western Cwm, and was now heading for Namche with the news? The scoundrel! Gripping my ice-axe firmly, like an irascible colonel about to deal with trespassers, I stumped heavily down the gully again, oblivious of any watching *yetis*. My goodness, I thought, whoever he is, he's making good time. He can certainly move! And as I watched the approaching figure I realized that this was no ordinary Sherpa, moving so swiftly and gracefully down the valley, swinging and buoyant, like some unspoilt mountain creature. A wide-brimmed hat! High reindeer boots! A smile that illuminated the glacier! An outstretched hand of greeting! Tenzing!

'Good gracious me, Tenzing! Haven't you walked far enough? Where in heaven's name are you off to now, like a bat out of hell?'

He took off his big hat, smiling still, and sat down upon a rock, while my excited Sherpas crowded round. He was going to the neighbouring village of Thamey, he said, to see his aged mother, who lived there. I was astonished at his freshness and strength. He looked rather older, I thought, than the day I had met him first, down the hill at Thyangboche; rather thinner, certainly; perhaps a little more assured, as if he had some inkling of things to come; but he was as lively and springy as ever, though only two days before he had hauled himself with such appalling labour to the top of the world.

He was going to rest and wash, and then traverse a neighbouring ridge towards his village. We had breakfast together, and I asked him if, as a souvenir of our meeting there, he had a photograph that he would sign for me. He pulled from his wallet a snapshot of himself with a number of little Tibetan terriers. 'Given me by the Dalai Lama,' he explained with pride, 'when I was in Lhasa with Professor Piccardi.' Taking a pen from his pocket, he slowly wrote his signature (the only word he could write) across the bottom of it and handed it to me with a self-deprecatory grin. The last I saw of him at Lobuje, he had stripped his lean, lithe body to the waist, and was soaping himself with water from a tin basin. It looked a chilly operation.

Out of the snow peaks we passed, and into the damp green alpine valley of Phalong Karpo. By now, I thought, my runner had presented my message to Mr. Tiwari, and if all went well it should go to Katmandu by the afternoon transmission. But who could tell what happened on the way? Had he been intercepted by unscrupulous rivals? Had he let me down, and found the ex-nuns of Thyangboche, or the *chang* of Namche, so enticing that he had long ago lost that precious dispatch? Had Mr. Tiwari rebuffed him? Or seen, with the quick flash of a policeman's eye, that the dispatch was not what it seemed to be?

Well, there were always the other runners, striding ahead of us on the road to Katmandu. That beguiling capital was now seething with rumours about Everest. Wild and wonderful reports were appearing in the press, and half the world believed that brief mendacious message, telling of the failure of the assault, which had reached us so impertinently at the moment of reunion. So I had my moments of anxiety as I hastened through the static yaks. At Base Camp I knew nobody had preceded me down the mountain. Now there were three men ahead of me carrying in their pockets the news of success. Only one thing comforted me, as I thought of the pleasant social encounters they might undergo in the course of the journey: not one of them knew what he was carrying!

The monks greeted us kindly at Thyangboche, and we rested for a moment on a low stone wall outside the monastery. Many were the friendly and keenly inquisitive divines and Sherpas who crowded around us there, with many a sharp insidious question. My Sherpas, thoroughly aware of the need for secrecy, just for a few more days, almost overdid the thing in their exaggerated expressions of conspiracy, their faces contorted with silence, their eyes twinkling, their fingers held to their lips, their cheeks bursting with suppressed laughter and information. We passed on our way intact.

A very good thing we did, for only a short way out of Thyangboche, on the track to Namche Bazar, I ran slap-bang into Peter Jackson, on his way home to the derelict villa he had rented from the monks. As we saw each other, in the dappled shade of the juniper trees, we both stopped dead in our tracks.

'Well, well,' said Jackson.

'Ho hum!' said I.

'Here you are then,' said Jackson.

'More or less,' said I.

'Weather's very pleasant, don't you think?'

'Not too bad.'

'Are you—er—leaving the mountain now?'

'Oh I've been up there so long, you know, I feel the need for a rest. It'll be nice to get down in the green again for a bit.'

'Hmm. Things going all right?'

'Not too badly.'

'Everybody all right?'

'More or less.'

'It'd be a pity if they didn't climb it this time.'

'A shame, a great shame. Still, there's always the French.'

'Well,' said Jackson.

'Ho ha!' said I.

And with a shake of the hand and a twisted smile at each other we parted, he to climb the hill to Thyangboche, I to continue my journey towards the valley. I hoped, in this brief and enigmatic exchange, to give him some vague impression that the expedition was not going too well, without actually telling him any fibs; in fact, he told me afterwards, I was not successful. My guarded reference to the French, I flattered myself, would imply that Hunt's expedition was at least preparing to leave the mountain to next year's challengers: but I forgot that if all these pre-monsoon assaults failed, there would certainly be another British attempt in the autumn. Jackson spotted this discrepancy in my innuendoes at once, and as he wandered back to his monastery fostered a niggling nebulous suspicion that Everest had been climbed.

But hey ho! I was past him safely; he still had no radio; and he would not hear the news, unless it spread from Tenzing's village, for another day or two. Soon we approached the grassy ridge that stood above Namche Bazar. A few men and women stood about there, doing obscure things with bits of wool, and four or five children ran about and made faces at us. I was afraid that news of our passing would be taken down to the village, or that some sharp eyes in upstairs windows would see my little caravan as it skirted the place. There was a long expanse of green open to view from the village, and this we crossed at the double, our bags and rucksacks swaying and bumping, my odd paraphernalia rattling, the older Sherpas wheezing heavily. Nobody emerged to intercept us, and soon we were moving through thick woods to the east of Namche and scrambling down a steep leafy slope to the Dudh Khosi, cool and creamy between the trees.

As we descended a strange and uncomfortable lassitude overcame me, the effect perhaps of de-acclimatization. I had been weak on the glacier high above; now I was not only weak, but intolerably lazy. I could hardly bring myself to move my limbs, or urge my lungs to operate; and often, as we made our way along the stream, I would take off my pack and sit down upon a rock, burying my head in my arms, trying to recover my resolution. It was too ridiculous. The path was easy, the country delightful; the monsoon was about to burst, and there was a smell of fresh moisture in the air; but there, it had been a long three months on Everest, and a long, long march from Lake Camp, and my body and spirit were rebelling.

It was evening now. The air was cool and scented. Pine trees were all about us again, and lush foliage, and the roar of the swollen river rang in our ears. On the west bank of the Dudh Khosi, about six miles south of Namche Bazar, there was a Sherpa hamlet called Benkar. There, as the dusk settled about us, we halted for the night. In a small square clearing among the houses Sonam set up my tent, and I erected the aerial of my radio receiver. The Sherpas, in their usual way, marched boldly into the houses round about and established themselves among the straw, fires, and potatoes of the upstairs rooms. Soon there was a smell of roasting and the fragrance of tea. As I sat outside my tent meditating, with only a few urchins standing impassively in front of me, Sonam emerged with a huge plate of scrawny chicken, a mug of *chang*, tea, chocolate, and *chuppatis*.

How far had my news gone, I wondered as I ate? Was it already winging its way to England from Katmandu; or was it still plodding over the Himalayan foothills in the hands of those determined runners? Would tomorrow, June 2, be both Coronation and Everest Day? Or would the ascent fall upon London later, like a last splendid chime of the Abbey bells? There was no way of knowing; I was alone in a void; the chicken was tough; the urchins unnerving; I went to bed.

But the morning broke fair. Lazily, as the sunshine crept up my sleeping-bag, I reached a hand out of my mummied wrappings towards the knob of the wireless. A moment of fumbling; a few crackles and hisses; and then the voice of an Englishman.

Everest had been climbed, he said. Queen Elizabeth had been given the news on the eve of her Coronation. The crowds waiting in the wet London streets had cheered and danced to hear of it. After thirty years of endeavour, spanning a generation, the top of the earth had been reached and one of the greatest of all adventures accomplished. This news of Coronation Everest (said that good man in London) had been first announced in a copyright dispatch in *The Times*.

I jumped out of my bed, spilling the bed-clothes about me, tearing open the tent-flap, leaping into the open in my filthy shirt, my broken boots, my torn trousers; my face was thickly bearded, my skin cracked with sun and cold, my voice hoarse. But I shouted to my Sherpas, whose bleary eyes were appearing from the neighbouring windows:

'Chomolungma finished! Everest done with! All okay!'

'Okay, sahib!' the Sherpas shouted back. 'Breakfast now?'

Far away in Westminster, as the notables prepared themselves, Field-Marshal Montgomery opened his newspaper that morning to read the news from Everest: so an adventure ended, crossed the continents, and joined the narratives of history.

Envoi

SURE ENOUGH, between the mountain and the mail my message leaked, and only its impenetrable code saved me from discomfiture. Some of those who saw its wording assumed it to be the herald of failure, and reported accordingly. One Indian fostered the theory (later published in a book) that it was not in code at all but that the subtle British, in one of their face-saving operations, had turned an announcement of impending defeat into the news of alleged victory. Everywhere people supposed that Everest had been climbed some days before, but that the news had been withheld to coincide with the Coronation.

The gossip faded, though, and the squabbles subsided. Everest became more than a national pride, or the possession of a privileged few. It took its place (if one may be a little sententious) among the triumphs of the human spirit, shared by all. For a year or two money was made from it, political hobby-horses were ridden, heroes were erected; publishers competed for its tales, and the cinema advertised the exploit with high-falutin' commentaries. A cheap and shoddy tarnish settled upon the adventure, like a rusting sea-mist upon silver.

But the thing grew with the years, and outdistanced its detractors, and became part of all our heritage, Easterners and Westerners, Communists and Capitalists, quiet men and adventurers. Which newspaper procured that triumphant message from the mountain? Nobody remembers, and all the others soon filched it anyway. Who stepped on the summit first? I have forgotten (and never asked). Were they British or Indian, those ultimate mountaineers, Buddhist or Christian, white or brown? Who cares? They reached the top of the world, and sent their delight not only to the Queen of England on her day of dedication, but to all the rest of us as well: a royal gift in every sense, our Coronation Everest.